"I think that a lot of girls, myself included, need to have the concepts that you mention in the book reiterated and reinforced. Deep down we already know these things (that's why I found myself saying, "oh yeah, that makes sense..."), but having them articulated on paper in front of us and being reinforced really makes it click. The other thing I really liked was the wittiness of the book! It really is a good read and kept my attention. I love the violin comparison too!!"

Karli, University of Toledo
Toledo, Ohio

"I like how positive you have made it. Relationships really are more than just "playing" games, that's where most go wrong. I think the parts that really catch my attention are those when you give insight into what the guys are thinking and their wants and needs. You being a male gives it credibility. When girls talk with their roommates, all we can do is guess what the heck is going through men's heads! College guys seem to be so wrapped up in school friends and partying that it is hard to catch their attention for more than just a short fling....and it is definitely hard to find guys that are good for more than just a short fling."

Caylyne, Butler University
Indianapolis, Indiana

"Fall in love with the wit and blue eyes and you get to find out about his bad features when your heart is wide open because your eyes were wide shut" I really like this quote. I think it's really smart. I personally learned this lesson several years ago, which I think is a much earlier age then for most. Unfortunately, I think there are a good number of people who go their whole lives, blindly ignoring this concept."

Karla, University of Tampa
Tampa, Florida

"One's philosophy is not best expressed in words; it is expressed in the choices one makes... and the choices we make are ultimately our responsibility." Eleanor Roosevelt

"This book would probably be most appropriate for undergraduate females looking for relationships. I would like to think women my age have learned most of its contents already through trial and error. For my part, I wish that I had received the knowledge this book contains when I was younger to avoid learning through personal experience. I think that your strategies empower women in regards to relationships, giving them more control and making them feel like they do and should have a say in what goes on with their significant other. At any rate, your book definitely puts the women in charge of dating, and if I ever have a daughter, I would strongly recommend that she read it."

Gwen, Michigan State University Grad Student
East Lansing, Michigan

"When I read this book I didn't think I had much else to learn about relationships, but it made me sit back and rethink everything. Finding a guy you want to be with isn't just about the initial attraction. If you want something to work you have to take a deeper look before you jump in head first. You explain a lot of things I knew some where in my subconscious, but now that I hear them coming from a guy, I'll believe them!"

Sarah, Albion College, Grad Student
Albion, Michigan

"When you choose your friends, don't be short-changed by choosing personality over character." W. Somerset Maugham

Empowering College Women

Strategies for Campus Relationships

Rick Becker

"100 Amazing Ideas to 'Amp-up' Your Best Game."

34 Opportunities - 30 Strategies - 36 Techniques

First Edition

ViolinPlay.com,™ LLC
Okemos, Michigan

Empowering College Women
Strategies for Campus Relationships
By Rick Becker

Published by: **ViolinPlay.Com LLC**
Post Office Box 1307
Okemos, MI 48805-1307
Order@CampusBliss.com   http://CampusBliss.com

ISBN 978-0-9778254-0-0   print English ed. softbound
ISBN 978-0-9778254-0-1   ebook English
ISBN 978-0-9778254-0-2   abook English sound file
SAN: 850-2625
                Library of Congress Cataloging-in-Publication Data
Becker, Rick.
Empowering college women : strategies for campus relationships / by Rick Becker. -- 1st ed.
p. cm.
Includes index.
ISBN-13: 978-0-9778254-0-0 (softbound)
ISBN-10: 0-9778254-0-X (softbound)

1. Man-woman relationships--United States.
2. Women college students--United States--Social life and customs.
3. Dating (Social customs)--United States.
I. Title.

HQ801.B43 2007   306.7'084'220973
QBI07-600120

CONTENTS

IV The Master Plan   "Instruction"

V The Date   "The Recital"

Quick Start – Jump to:

Section V - Dating and Section VIII – Sweet Relationships
Also helpful lists for rating personality traits in the back.

Short on time and patience, frustrated and need answers now? Chances are you have problems with guys because you pick the wrong ones. Dating can make you crazy. So whether you're between relationships and a bit battle-scarred or in one that doesn't feel right here's how to pick a winner and how you should think about the one that is only slightly wrong you may be with now. Not in a hurry but have ADD like me? Hop around wherever your curiosity takes you. Not in a hurry and remarkably normal? Begin here. ☺

Preface

At 26 I helped start a large college nightclub. It was debatable whether we were in the bar, entertainment or relationship business. In retrospect I realize now we were in the *relationship* business. For twenty years I observed our patrons' and particularly our staff's actions and reactions to forming, evolving and ending their romantic couplings.

This book is about some of my amazing discoveries that naturally occur between townies and students, management and staff, wait staff and bartenders, customers and security, office and operations, men and women and ultimately, before the night was over, between the overly passionate, the mysteriously sober, and the obnoxiously intoxicated. It was a confluence of desire, decorum and de beer. I'm a fix-it kind of guy and since I like to get personally involved, I did. I soon realized it was key to gain everyone's perspective in a relationship question and, when possible, learn their talents and skill set, discover their passions and career goals and then try to understand their big picture.

Over time I attempted to learn each individual staff's talents, beliefs and feelings and then help translate them into possible future career job descriptions. Idle conversations with students, whether staff or patron, nearly always focused on them and what unique resources they were blessed with and how much fun it would be to imagine centering their lives around those passions instead of locking them away simply because life is not supposed to be fun. "Play is fun. Work is work." So the myth goes.

You might imagine how discovering people's passions and then possibility-thinking their life goals, over so many years, slowly evolved into two of my core competencies. (Focused repetition can be a powerful learning tool.) Sure, sometimes it was just offering a listening ear to a person in conflict or to one experiencing chaos in their life. Student life is filled with crossroads and many of them are being witnessed for the first time. Someone who has viewed how other students have reacted can often be a help.

Over time I collected techniques I saw working in relationships and applied them to our staff. I even took ideas proven in business and suggested them in relationships. The truly amazing relationship strategies and techniques are all here. Most have far reaching applications with friends and workers! All of these ideas are time tested by me and work amazingly well a very high percentage of the time. Get ready for results. Prepare to practice though. Practice guarantees very high percentage, *amazing* results.

I have divided the ideas (short essays) into three types: *opportunity* – what naturally and often powerfully wants to occur when certain circumstances are present; *strategies* – methods for using these amazing opportunities to your mutual advantage; *techniques* – your actions necessary to achieve the best possible result as quickly as possible, again to your mutual advantage.

Some of these techniques are *deceptively* simple. Somewhere in these writings you will hear yourself mutter, "I need a sledge hammer right now, not this Q-Tip!" Ah…for sure, but given the combination to a bank safe… you could quicker open it by turning the dial with a cotton swab than by smashing it with a hammer.

Do not equate complex with effective.

I have seen a lot of sledge hammer techniques attempted but nothing compares to the diesel-train stopping power of a clever lady's sly smile, subtle whisper, well timed wink or sweet touch. Simple concentrates power.

Rick Becker

Acknowledgments

A toast to all you angels, seen and unseen who visit our lives and guide our senses to find the way. Admittedly speed is not your strong suit but I am reminded that the best experience often demands waiting for the catalysts before the teaching can occur. I imagine my maker sits in the rear of the canoe steering as I sit forward paddling. I know that if the scenery is not to my liking I should paddle faster. So here's to You who cloak Your presence with the majesty of the universe. "Nice work if you can get it." (…and you thought humor came from?)

Next I want to thank the girls and the guys at the club and restaurant for sharing their best and worst relationship experiences over the years. Some were customers but most were staff. To my bartender Kelly Vermetti: thank you for demonstrating what recognition looks and sounds like. "See how you are?"

Thanks also to numerous women who informed my thinking, edited and shaped the text and format: Kendrah, Stephanie, Beth, and Amanda. The beautiful cover is Cathi Stevenson's of Dartmouth, Nova Scotia. Last minute details came from Bobbie Graham in Quebec and Alan Gadny in California – two pro book shepherds. Also to Dan Poynter, the guy that wrote the book for self publishers. Finally to my family: "Thank you for your support."

I dedicate these writings to my father and mother who gave me a sense of kindness and outreach to others that stands today as a core principle of my life and this book. Walking through his large factory as a boy I frequently heard people say that they hoped I would grow up to be just like him and my grandfather. I got my earliest inspiration from sincere, kind, genuine, amazingly accomplished people.

And to you the college woman: "You carry the torch. May it illuminate your path and reveal possibilities that will empower your uniqueness to rise to its highest and best use and as well as those you coach and cheer for." I pass the torch forward to you."

Warning – Disclaimer

This book is intended to provide information on self improvement and relationships. It is offered with the understanding that the publisher and author are not engaged in rendering psychological, medical or other professional services.

Achieving self improvement and creating strong relationships is not a quick, overnight exercise but a life-long process. This book attempts to supply strategies and techniques calculated to accelerate the learning process.

The purpose of this manual is to educate and entertain. The author and publisher shall have neither liability nor responsibility to any person, persons or entity with respect to any loss or damage, caused or alleged to have been caused, directly or indirectly, by the information contained in this book.

Section I

Playing a Relationship like a What?
"Fiddling Around"

Introduction
Harmony
Harmony & Recognition
Fiddling Around with Metaphors
Coaching College Men

A person once armed with knowledge of the natural power they possess to foster and nurture their own as well as another's fulfillment …becomes a formidable ally in life's grand adventure.

HARMONY

LOVE is the child of harmony.
Harmony comes with accommodation.
Accommodation begins with recognition.
Recognition confers admiration & respect.
Admiration & respect build self confidence.
Self confidence is the engine of accomplishment.
Accomplishment is self actualizing.
Self actualization is fulfillment.
Fulfillment is harmony.
Harmony is bliss.

Introduction

1

Strategy

Y ou will be learning the most powerful techniques for attracting men, meeting them, sorting them out, and beginning a friendship which may cement the foundation of a relationship that will bond you to each other - permanently. That bonding influence is produced by your attention to one another's intimate, personal details like talents and life goals and your ability to coach and cheer each other on to maximize and attain them. You can become a powerful team and produce such results in one another that it creates a harmonic relationship and makes you think, "This truly is amazing, this thing I share with this person. I feel so empowered! We really compliment each other."

You will accomplish all this when you learn to empower your essence, amplify your unique traits and special talents, and begin utilizing your power to recognize the essence of others, cheer it on, and feel the respect and confidence it creates in both of you. Start by maximizing the elements of attraction. A dynamite smile comes first, and it's easy to train those muscles to respond quickly and effortlessly. A natural smile is nice, but there's something even more important than that. It's the "I think you're just great" smile. It is recognition and admiration wrapped into one, and people just eat it up – especially men, when you shine it at them. I will show you how to acquire that look while walking to class.

Next, you will study what it is about people that you truly admire. Then you begin sharing it with them - when the moment is right. Once you have practiced complimenting people and have become comfortable and encouraged with how they respond to your recognition of some valuable trait you will be ready to use this technique with college men. Men love recognition, and when you begin complimenting them on their best features – not just their physical assets, you will have their *undivided* attention. With practice you will quickly acquire techniques which will reveal and celebrate the wonderment of talents, skills and positive personality features instead of the usual good looks, high I.Q or wealth.

When recognition occurs, you will find admiration and respect close behind. Positive, attractive energy is generated. Men begin appearing and shyness disappears. Your confidence expands as people open themselves up to your simple yet perceptive observations that leave them feeling better for having bumped into you. Your smile transmits genuine admiration and respect. Your body chemistry is boosted. You feel a lot better more often.

Once a college man appears that you like, you ask him to meet you for coffee/soda so that you can have a deeper look before going out with him. You will peer into his past and learn about some unique achievement and feel his passion and energy. You will learn how to casually assess a man so that entire cross sections of him are revealed. You will sense strong, telling images of his courage, integrity, wisdom, practicality, honesty, ingenuity, wisdom, patience and kindness. It's all there to admire and evaluate as you ask about his favorite "war stories" (passion), grandest dreams for the future (imagination, optimism) and finally who he most admires as a role model (inspiration, values). A few lattes/red pops later that afternoon and you'll know whether he is worth hanging out with.

After you begin screening your prospects, it's unlikely that you'll experience a bad date but, just in case, you'll learn how to deal with people chaos when it rears it's ugly head. For the most part relationships will begin improving because your decisions now focus on heart and mind instead of eyes and shoulders. He will now know when he is real for you when you validate his role as "the one." Once that occurs, you will work with each other's talents and dreams to craft a plan to make them happen. Cheering and coaching another to their dream is very intimate stuff. Every day witnesses their greatness appearing and every day you capture those moments and verbally celebrate them. "See how you are - you amaze me!"

Recognizing relationships early on that are nothing more than natural chemistry, physical attraction, or simple coincidence is key. Relationships that are built on friendship with a central theme of mutual empowerment are the real power play. Teaching the other person empowering techniques, first by example and then by instruction, ensures they will be equipped to coach your best game when you turn their attention to your dreams recognizing your individual essences, applauding their appearance, and empowering each other's plan to achieve their unique destiny is what you want for each other. This means learning to coach and men love to be coached by positive minded, goal setters.

Great coaching requires behavior modification techniques that focus on positive *what should be*, and never negative *what is* or *was*. Techniques that always uplift and never degrade are what you'll learn here. Subtle techniques using body language, vocal tones and touch produce results that will astound you. Moving close to him and speaking in hushed tones capture his attention and a soft touch while speaking *electrifies* the message. Summoning repeating, psychological forces like these to overwrite minor recurring behavior flaws ensures lasting, positive change that easily moves the relationship along your dream paths .

If it sounds like girl power…just keep reading. The topics that follow will develop the concepts, describe the strategies, reveal the tricks and traps, quote famous people, role play the dialogue and explain how I came to feel so sure about motivating college men. Knowing how to motivate college men is an important resource, but taking ownership of your dreams, believing they are worth chasing and using teamwork as an accelerator is a far greater resource. This is about your total empowerment.

Trends, fads, crazes, and rages in western culture like dress, food and music are always changing because sameness is boredom. Being stimulated visually, orally, audibly, tactilely and olfactoraly is a task we necessarily assign ourselves to avoid that boredom. Necessarily what is *hot* today is *so not* tomorrow. Dealing with fads will be left to others. This book is about the stuff that doesn't change with fashion because the trend is always about empowering one's talents and charting an amazing life for one's self. The human mechanism responds predictably to appreciation and respect when approached responsibly with sensitivity and feeling. Human beings evolve predictably faster when encouraged, empowered and enabled. Tastes change, hunger remains. Tell that self of yours to super-size a heaping portion of your best stuff and learn to find somebody you can really cook-up a great life with. No bun intended.

Harmony

2

Opportunity

E mpowerment thrives on all sorts of dynamic interactions that occur when we set off the amazing chain reaction below that enables it. Here are the natural laws of human psychology we'll use to direct you and your man's lives to your grandest visions. Here are the irrefutable facts of life human beings observe. When the facts are assembled in this particular order one can sense a building of one upon the other. A formula for empowerment might be postulated. Empowering an individual, a couple, a group finds a pathway to realizing its goal. For instance, begin with recognition and follow it just to accomplishment. Can you see why a guy who admires you would prize your partnering with him if he had a great dream?

"Principles for the Development of a Complete Mind: Study the science of art. Study the art of science. Develop your senses - especially learn how to see. Realize that everything connects to everything else." Leonardo DaVinci

HARMONY

LOVE is the child of harmony.
Harmony comes with accommodation.
Accommodation begins with recognition.
Recognition confers admiration & respect.
Admiration & respect build self confidence.
Self confidence is the engine of accomplishment.
Accomplishment is self actualizing.
Self actualization is fulfillment.
Fulfillment is harmony.
Harmony is bliss.

Harmony & Recognition
3
Strategy

R eal love requires recognizing and appreciating another's beliefs and values, their virtues and character traits...and communicating yours to them for their appreciation. Once this is accomplished, you make room for their issues. If you can enjoy their positives and accommodate their negatives you have a basis for friendship.

Friendship is the precursor to enduring love.

You first like and admire each other enough to ignore stuff that would irritate you in another. Your accommodation of another's issues – good and bad – creates trust, admiration and respect. These in turn develop a powerful engine of accomplishment. Coaching each other to evolve into your best selves (self actualization) is the goal.

Develop the necessary set of skills (skill set) to sort out the college men that are right for you. Be smart with your selection so that harmony and possibly romantic love can grow without having to deal with confusion, conflict and ultimately chaos. Fall in love with the next cool looking guy that asks for your number, skip the interview process at the Union or coffee shop, proceed directly on a series of laughter filled dates, and you are statistically doomed to heartache and frustration.

People are complex. You are a person. He is too. Fall in love with the wit and blue eyes and you get to find out about his bad features when your heart is wide open because your eyes were wide shut. You couldn't wait to go out with him, you recall. All that changed minutes into the date. Choosing the right college man requires learning first how to choose and then apply those principles in your relationships with others.

What are college men looking for in you? Their goal is much like yours. They're looking for a partner who bothers to learn and understand why they believe and feel as they do about the passions that drive them. If you can become passionate about them for who they are, they can admire and respect you, passionately, in return.

This concept works both ways. The key is to work the principle, to put it in motion and that is the substance of these writings – drawing on the deep wellsprings of human feelings to form empowering alliances that drive behavior toward accomplishing our wonderful dreams. Our passions are the jet fuel. Cheering and coaching are the guidance systems you'll learn to enable each other's best behavior and morph dreams into reality.

The object is to help breathe life into each other's dreams by targeting passions which power the baby-steps – one at a time, day after day – that move us along our dream paths, amazed and fulfilled at how our talents have been harnessed and our joys are being realized.

…drawing on the deep wellsprings of human feelings to form empowering alliances that drive behavior toward accomplishing our wonderful dreams.

Fiddling Around with Metaphors
4
Opportunity

Our Metaphor, the Violin

Take the violin...the elements seem obvious enough. Strings of different grades are connected to an acoustically hollow frame and then to an arm where tightening devices are mounted. When tension is put on the strings and they are tweaked, they vibrate to create different tones. One day I was struck with the similarity between an individual's "inner strings" – one's personality traits, and a violin's strings. I was then, of course, compelled to extend the metaphor to music and relationships and was amazed at the efficacy of their parallels. What a handy crutch I thought. Thus we have the world of violins and music popping up from time to time throughout the book. As I am not a music person the comparisons I attempt should easily resonate with you. Okay – that was weak but....

I say all of this to make a simple point. You have a unique set of features that cannot be seen, even with medical imaging devices. This set of features – talents, character, personality, and instincts – while invisible to technology, are obvious to the studied observer. So for purposes of illustration we'll refer to the mental stuff that makes us unique as the "string set." Playing his strings and coaching him to play yours in a clever and practiced way, consistently over time, should produce for you and yours the phenomenon known as harmony. Love is the child of harmony. Harmony is bliss.

"The metaphor is perhaps one of man's most fruitful potentialities. Its efficacy verges on magic, and it seems a tool for creation which God forgot inside one of His creatures when He made him". Jose Ortega y Gasset

Coaching College Men
5
Strategy

College men appreciate their coaches. They regard positive minded coaches with high esteem. They know that a coach empowers. Translate the nurturing feature of your personality into empowerment in your everyday life and you'll have a lot of men watching you closely. Coaches have a way of getting the best out of their athletes by encouraging, praising, guiding, cheering and believing in them. When he experiences you compliment, encourage and cheer the people you come across in everyday life, he will appreciate you and want to study you whenever you are present. You will be stunningly attractive with or without cosmetic enhancements. Men love empowering women.

Why do you suppose so many college guys are so into sports? The answer is passion. The fact that it comes packaged as action shouldn't mislead you. Take away the passion from his action and his interest falls apart faster than the "my dog ate the book report" excuse did in high school. Want to get his attention? Focus on passion – his, yours, theirs –and you've got his attention. What thrills him: creation, knowledge, people, process, harmony? Discovering and focusing conversation, activities and goal setting on the application of these passions will get his attention, and keep it.

> "Admiration is a very short-lived passion that immediately decays upon growing familiar with its object, unless it be still fed with fresh discoveries, and kept alive by a new perpetual succession of miracles rising up to its view."
> Joseph Addison

When attempting to quickly understand a person's passions, it is important to hear their "war" stories – the "them against the odds and how they fared" story. While you're discovering who this person is you should also listen to their grandest dream of what they hope to become. Those two stories, the "best of me" and "best I hope to become" stories, will shed a lot of light on who this person is. A final perspective to add to the mix is the role model – who is inspirational to him?

If you want to help empower this person, you want to glimpse their passion and learn what they hope to be, what they see in who they admire, and imagine whether you want to get on board this dream. You will learn their beliefs and values, gauge their skills and discover their virtues, like courage, honesty and patience. You will know what drives them and what distorts them. Here is a peak at the control panel. This is where you cheer and coach from.

Men love empowering women.
They motivate us to pursue and achieve what we are passionate about.

"Without passion man is a mere latent force and possibility,
like the flint which awaits the shock of the iron
before it can give forth its spark."
Henri Frederic Amiel

Section II

Recognition
The Strings

The Recognition Family
The Most Powerful Compliments
Natural Opiates
Chaos & Harmony
Life's Little Sticky Notes
The Artist's Vision
People Chaos
What Needs Accommodation
Hidden Agendas
Mission Statement
Fools' Gold
First Goal
Fire Escape
Screening
Certain Failure
Stop Being a Freshman

HARMONY

LOVE is the child of harmony.
Harmony comes with accommodation.
Accommodation begins with recognition.
Recognition confers admiration & respect.
Admiration & respect build self confidence.
Self confidence is the engine of accomplishment.
Accomplishment is self actualizing.
Self actualization is fulfillment.
Fulfillment is harmony.
Harmony is bliss.

The Recognition Family
6
Opportunity

Recognition might mean appreciation, approval, affirmation, awareness, authentication, applause, respect, valuation, credit. All are positive; all are nourishing. But recognition has supernatural powers too, that you will learn to use to enable and empower yourself and others to achieve a potpourri of dreams. Caution: recognition, properly dispensed, will release "feel-good" opiates into the bloodstream. These powerful, all natural drugs can change a person's behavior and overwrite bad habits with the creation of positive new habits. This stunning discovery we will apply at every turn.

Vocal recognition of character ranks highest in impact because it penetrates directly to the "self." We can fake our behavior, forge our looks and massage our personality, but character is our core. A cross section of us reveals some key components – beliefs and values, integrity - how closely we adhere to our own rules and as well, society's, and of course, our talents, the things we're effortlessly good at and other's best efforts never seem to equal.

It's great to get a compliment on how nice we look. Someone is saying our interpretation of our appearance (make-up, outfit, color, design, choice of jewelry) is pleasing to them. When we get a compliment on an act or achievement, someone is saying that we have chosen an appropriate behavior for the occasion. When someone compliments us on a talent or a character trait, however, they are complimenting us on who we are, not just on what we did. Recognizing and applauding another's talent or character trait unleashes admiration and respect for both people. The target gets a courage boost – for however they wish to spend it. This awesome phenomenon will be responsible for a handsome portion of the empowerment success you will achieve.

"There are two things that people want more than sex and money –
recognition and praise."
Mary Kay Ash, founder Mary Kay Cosmetics

The Most Powerful Compliment
7
Strategy

There is no more powerful compliment than when one peers into our soul and finds our self pleasing and appropriate. We all want to believe that we belong, have value, and are capable of accomplishing something of worth. This type of compliment is truly remarkable for the chain reaction that it can start.

It becomes obvious in time that everyone's favorite topic of conversation is them self and, most specifically, their talents. Everybody has discovered one thing at which few can match them; so while getting acquainted with people, draw those things out. Learn their favorite stories, discover their role model, and maybe even catch a glimpse of their ultimate dream. You will mine this raw material for appreciation and comment. This is the stuff of his passions. This is where his heart dwells. Mentioning any of it guarantees his attention. Compliments that are well thought out will have powerful effects. Use them to empower the mini-steps to his dreams and you will have a formidable ally.

> "Praise, when it is not deserved, is the severest satire and abuse."
> Lord Chesterfield

Everybody knows what makes them special, even if they don't know they know. The answers are stored in their brain's Favorite Stories File. Sit around a campfire and watch them come dancing out of people's heads! Everyone has a never ending storybook of tales that demonstrate their victories and their vanquishments. As they share their passionate story, you watch for clues that reveal their talents, character, beliefs and values.

> "It's good to shut up sometimes." Marcel Marceau, French Mime

Once they finish their story, your line of conversation should pursue the talent or skill their story illustrates. Remark by doing a little summary which lets them know you were into what they were saying and understood it. From your perspective, think, "If I get it wrong, they'll correct me and just proceed." No problem. Try correlating the story to their major in school or similar interest.

Me: "So what I heard you say in that great story about drawing and sending cartoons of certain professor's behavior to your college paper's editor is that you really get off spoofing authority. And I think you mentioned you're a Poli-Sci major but you haven't got a clue what you'll use it for, is that right?"

Her: "Yea. Our family is all about politics, so I think growing up with it just made it a natural choice."

Me: "So just how good is your cartooning?"

Her: "Oh I'm good, but I'm not into comic books or whimsical social commentary like the funny papers."

Me: "I can picture you being paid to raise some serious hell on the editorial pages of a big city newspaper as a syndicated political cartoonist though. I definitely sense a strong attitude. Is that an impossible thought?"

Her: "Well, my father wants me to be a political consultant with his brother's firm at the state capitol, but it sounds pretty boring, I admit. I'm kind of the black sheep of the family – sort of an independent spirit. I can't really picture myself telling somebody the right things to say to get elected. In fact, that kind of social hypocrisy makes me ill just thinking about it."

Me: "Oh, well that rules out political satire then, doesn't it?"

Her: (Wheels start turning in her head. A look of mischief comes over her face) "I've gotta go punch in, I'm third on. I think my uncle hates you!"

Natural Opiates
8
Opportunity

W hen someone we admire observes our noteworthy act and vocalizes a compliment about our inner qualities, it does more than give us a head rush. Accurate observations about a person's positive personality traits reinforce the beliefs that sponsored that behavior. That means we can expect more of that behavior if we will just bother to water that flower we so admire. Don't look at yourself as a brown-noser, tossing around compliments that cause people to blush, but as an empowerer giving nourishment to personalities hungry to climb the ladder of self accomplishment - if not from you, then from whom?

Belief reinforcement strengthens our resolve to rise to higher and better uses for ourselves as well. Self belief translates to confidence. Confidence is our passport through the valley of fear, the future, and the unknown and, worst of all, self doubt. Fear of failure is our worst enemy. The journey to our highest and best use requires self confidence and fully utilizing our best stuff, our talents. Risking our best stuff in life's challenge is not for the weak hearted. We all need help and plenty of recognition of our talents and the daily challenges they meet. We're talking sharing and caring about what makes the other so special and unique. We're talking personality strengthening exercises required here. Self doubt is the hobgoblin of the successful as well as the failed – we all need positive reinforcement.

"People must help one another; it is nature's law." LaFontaine

Now that you're adding recognition to your bag of tricks, you've got the key starter ingredient needed to be a formidable ally, teacher, coach, facilitator, empowerer and master best friend. You've heard that every good relationship's partners learn to give and take, but that's just basic balance in the getting and having part. The growth hormone is the confidence building nourishment each of you adds to help enable the other's dreams.

Remember that while nature provides a free dose of endorphins to jump-start every new relationship, they soon fade like starter fertilizer and your enthusiasm for your guy, and he for you, soon must generate its own endorphins. It's why relationships grow tired. You better know how to keep those great feelings flowing, or you're going to feel like a musician with just the first page of music and a whole concert to go. Empowering each other is the stuff that great relationships are made of. "Behind every great man there's a great woman." You've heard that one. We're just adding *recognition for your side of the dream* and *his support of it* to this old maxim to empower your greatness.

Unlike most men you already know how capable your female body is of producing hormones that control mood and attitude. Men appreciate testosterone and its ability to build muscle mass but as far as other hormones and their effects on us we are usually oblivious. We know how we feel very differently when confronted by extreme circumstances like aggression or love. We don't realize that our bodies have secreted certain chemicals and the surge we feel is "drug" induced.

The subtle techniques I will teach you release secretions that are very effective at directing behavior. On the surface if sounds like no big deal. Below the surface it's a different story. Your well timed compliment or wink has the hitting power of a football thrown at his chest. All of my techniques provoke euphoric feelings in men. My strategy is to double and triple team these feelings to get amazing results out of your guy – once you really feel that he's a quality match for you.

Accurate observations about a person's positive personality traits reinforce the beliefs that sponsored those noteworthy acts.

Chaos & Harmony
9
Opportunity

Harmony and a little chaos are the reality and natural state of existence. Observe the soil, as it parts its tiny granules to allow a fine strand of an emerging plant to rise to meet the sunshine. Its ability to conduct heat signaled the seed; its porous nature allowed the water to penetrate the surface to germinate the seed; its firmness will support the roots as the plant ascends in height. Where the soil refuses to accommodate the seed, it will turn to the wind, the animals and the birds for new geography in a relentless process to find accommodating conditions. We are a part of existence ("I think, therefore I am!"). It's not a large leap to declare that harmony is the natural state of our existence too. Love needs a warm and fuzzy nest to grow in, and a state of harmony is the soil of our soul.

Chaos – like when the car won't start *and* you're already late for a quiz. You reach for your cell and your class notes fall in the puddle. This is a major detour from *the plan*. This is chaos. Interruptions are not appreciated, especially when there's a time value on that progress. Taking time out to find a ride when yours dies, suffering the look and attitude of a prof who doesn't tolerate lateness before a quiz, notes that will have to be copied or repurchased – these are not the features of harmony.

"Concordia discors." (Harmony in discord) Horace

If our natural state of being is harmony, how come life for you is full of so many nasty little moments? Welcome to the planet. Chaos is part of the natural order of things. People and animals are the only ones that seem to get an attitude about it. Things tend to bump into one another all the time in an effort to fit in, be a part of what is, be accepted. Not everything can be accepted and shuffled into the status quo, but that doesn't stop all sorts of things from trying. It's part of the process of natural selection. In order to be selected, something has gotta give, make space, accommodate. Like people in an elevator shifting to make room for the sweet little old lady with too much perfume, you do a little shift and gasp for a fresh breath of air.

Life's Little Sticky Notes
10
Technique

C haos and accommodation seem to be willing partners in life's little dance. In fact, chaos plays an important part in the dance of your particular life. Were it not for chaos, your behavior would be much different because chaos represents the consequences of ill-fitting, ill-timed, ill-suited choices. Your memory stores these chaotic consequences and provides reminders of them under similar situations in the hope that you'll not tempt chaos again.

The next time a quiz is announced, your mind darts to the car battery that failed and the thought that it was time to replace it. You decide to get another one after class and maybe look at a waterproof folder for notes, too. Your recognition of pain and pleasure are necessary for averting further episodes not to your liking.

Adapt, adjust, reorganize, substitute, restyle, and/or evolve are the choices we can make once we understand that we must change to achieve a goal.

You elect to deal with your problems, accepting that which you cannot change, by making calculated concessions to them. That battery was just going to get weaker with time, and rain puddles are a permanent hazard. So, recognize what needs to be integrated into your plan so that you can proceed along your path and meet your goals.

You've learned to make concessions to the laws of physics, accommodating everything from gravity to the extra concentration necessary to successfully manipulate a top-heavy slice of jellied toast with one hand while painting a toenail with the other. Not recognizing what needs to be accommodated can create pain, you've learned, and history likes to repeat itself. It will allow you to stub your toes in the dark as often as you care to repeat the mistake.

Artfully accommodating what we recognize as obstacles in our path is how we navigate life's little tributaries. We cross vast oceans the same way.

We learn to fix things at the first sign of weakness or watch them surprise us at the worst possible time. That little hole in your best outdoor sweater needs a stitch in the underarm before the toboggan party this afternoon. It plans a bigger coming out party later tonight for you.

Let's hear it for you for every time in the past and every time in the future that you reacted or will react *in time* to life's subtle clues that signal a call to arms – and not just the ones that emerge from holes in sweaters in public. It may be true that some people are clueless. Obviously you are not one of them. So here's to you.

Artfully accommodating what we recognize as obstacles in our path is how
we navigate life's little tributaries.

The Artist's Vision
11
Strategy

Your personal vision of life should be one of attempting to exhaust your talents at every opportunity in the pursuit of fulfilling your potential. You are the artist of your own portrait; you are the scriptwriter of your own videography; so also can you be the conductor of your own concert. Your mate can either be part of your journey to that fulfillment or part of the problem you encounter on the way.

Your knack for picking valid solutions will determine your comfort level in life. Your effectiveness in selecting a mate will determine not only the comfort level of your relationship, but also the degree of your fulfillment. Plan to be serious about your analysis. Hold really good interviews (coffees) and only good guys will hold you!

You are the Producer/Director of your autobiography as much before the words are written as after. You actually help configure your life and its circumstances based on your opinions, tastes and philosophy. As these three viewpoints shift with experience, you shift too. You evolve. Your target is? The highest and best use of you – your essence – and your character, talent, and attitude is your focus.

Wouldn't it be great to have a friend that looked after your evolution, cheered you along, helped you set goals that were purely and only all about you? Wouldn't it be fun to choose a path that aimed squarely at your deepest curiosities and desires? Find someone who can get serious and view themselves in a coaching role in your life. After all, you are that serious about reaching your dreams aren't you?

How silly would it be to screen for people with dreams you can appreciate and who could feel the same about yours? What if that person would be fun to coach, too, and would actually let you help them discover and pursue their grandest dreams? Would it be worth being especially wary of prospects that don't have the tools to work on your dreams?

What if someone especially attractive came along? Would you still keep them if they didn't "get" your dream or theirs was not to your liking? How attractive would they be then?

It's good to be aware of just what all you're going to need in this guy you are taking along on your life voyage. Cheering and coaching would be two things to try on him for size. How about imagination? Can he imagine you doing your grandest dream? What level of enthusiasm does your dream produce in his mind?

What parts is he not talking about - the moving, the career, the family, the settling down, the house, the kids, the no kids, the no house but several condos? Are you carefully watching and listening to what he has to say, or are you humming a tune, tapping your foot and wondering how good a kisser he is? Hello?

Your mate can either be part of your journey to that fulfillment or part of the problem you encounter on the way.

Find someone who can get serious and view themselves in a coaching role in your life. After all, you are that serious about reaching your dreams aren't you?

People Chaos
12
Strategy

T he good news: forewarned, is forearmed. The bad news: some guys are like some gals - they are not accommodators. They never learned how to give and take. They don't play nice. They can't be taught harmony. They are users and discarders. They'll flash a smile, melt your heart, trigger your endorphins, use ya, abuse ya, and be gone. These guys, like their female counterparts, are to be avoided as soon as they rear their ugly behavior. If you don't spot them, your friends probably will.

Learn to listen to the people who already love you, particularly if a number of them harp on an issue. Your love-spawned endorphins don't serve you well when they absorb the pain and anesthetize you to what you should be feeling from the behavior of an idiot, while your friends go blue in the face screaming wildly, "You are CRAZY to be with this person!"

One day, you suddenly wake-up, years from now - let's hope you're not pregnant again - thinking maybe divorce really is the only answer. Your decision, your pain. Cut your losses early while you are in college and your brain can still reject messages from your heart; not later with babies and a mortgage. Listen to your friends; they all can't be wrong. Remember, "…if two speak thus, purchase a saddle for thyself." (More about idiots later)

"If one should say to thee, thou art a donkey, do not mind; if two speak thus, purchase a saddle for thyself."
Midrash (4th cent B.C.-A.D. 12th cent) Rabbinical writings

What Needs Accommodation
13
Technique

G oals and the next steps necessary to reach them call for priority handling. These *next* steps are critical. Dreams ride on their backs. These steps are critical to the goal. It's called the "critical path." Getting to that quiz was critical because it won't come to you. You need the points for the class, the class for the major, the major for graduation, graduation for the career (after all – you're trying to get a life!).

It wasn't critical that you take *your* car, however. Somebody else's car or the bus would have worked. My point: when you're in a relationship and you find yourself in a heated argument about something that has nothing to do with the next step on the critical path to a life goal, calm down. You are about achieving your dream and facilitating other's.

If one or both of you always need to have your way, *then* you have a serious impediment in the accommodation mechanism of your relationship. Let's recognize that right away. How do you expect to play a duet when one of you doesn't want to follow the music and let the other play their part? Remember, sometimes we take turns. So, he wants to go there, she wants to go here.

Questions like these should be illuminated with an eye to each other's personal beliefs and values, talent issues and life goals. If you don't do violent movies, that's something that will decide in advance what movies the two of you will or will not go to. If you're a Textile/Merchandising major, a particular film set in a period could shed light on fashions you should know about - that's a career issue that might be a "decider."

My point here is that sometimes we can feed two birds with one bean; so why not combine career and entertainment when possible? That's why he needs to be an accommodator. Certainly he should be able to find this flick a little entertaining also. It shouldn't be a total dud.

Taste and career issues indicate what you do and where you go, or you toss a coin. Just recognize that certain issues carry more weight than others and both parties should be willing to give in for good reasons. If he can't play like that, then he is not a team player; so take your ball and go home. Don't try to fix him if he always resists your opportunities for advancement and always makes a big deal out of what plainly is junk entertainment.

Professionals attempt to fix people. Don't attempt being a Fixer. Violin fixing is a trade unto itself. It's a whole plate full. Besides, can't you afford a guy that's not a "fixer-upper." Do not let anyone convince you that you only deserve dysfunctional people or that you can find harmony with someone who is not willing to grow with you. There is something much better in store for you than that, but it is up to you to recognize it.

"Don't compromise yourself; you are all you've got."
Janis Joplin

Hidden Agendas
14
Strategy

I ncidentally, a clue that sometimes helps explain why you seem to prefer certain types of men, is your perception of your father. We tend to project the image of the opposite sex parent, whether good or bad, onto others. This may determine who we are attracted to, consciously or not. Unfortunately, you may only find yourself comfortable around types you are familiar with, sort of like home. Take a picture of your father's ways and plug them in as answers to why your friends pester you about your choice of men: "Dad is an alcoholic who mistreats mom and I always seem drawn to the 'bad boys.'" Or, "Sure, Dad is a womanizer, but why do I always hook up with guys who cheat on me?" Deep in your brain, there's a magnet attached to a little memory chip that needs to have some reprogramming by a trained professional. You need to be reassured this is a shortcoming in the human imprinting experience shared by millions of men and women over thousands of years. So get yourself fixed, or get yourself fixed! We don't need more of these guys. They give the rest of us a bad name.

"No change of circumstances can repair a defect of character."
Ralph Waldo Emerson

Mission Statement
15
Strategy

Creating your mission statement and his involves:

1) Recognizing his character, personality, and talents.
2) Directing his attention to recognize yours.
3) Communicating your dreams and how each of you plans
   to reach them.
4) Learning if each of you is willing to coach and cheer the
   other in the support of their dreams.

C oaching and cheering is the PIN code and the password that unlock
the fast track to fulfillment. Two people can reach their dreams more
quickly by coaching and cheering each other's individual projects than by
working alone. However, you must be motivated, aware and receptive to
each other's support. You don't work on "your relationship." You each work
on empowering each other's personal dreams, and your relationship
strengthens as the by-product.

Two empowering people are more strongly attracted to each other than two
self-coached people who observe each other's goals passively.

Sharing the outstanding features of each other's personality and the
everyday achievements they produce enables you to do more than just assess
whether you like each other as people. It gives your relationship the added
feature of demonstrating to each other right away the beneficial advantages
of staying together. Opportunities constantly present themselves to help
each other. How many times have you picked up an item at the store or
emailed a link to someone you knew would appreciate it because they had
shared their dream and you felt this would advance them on their trek?
Remember how amazed they reacted? You did more than provide a dream
resource - you set off a chain reaction of harmony.

Synergy is a beautiful thing. Feel the bliss. Throw back your hair and feel the sunshine of the Caribbean, feel the white powder sand beach between your toes. Are your ready for this – keep reading. It will begin to reveal its compounding effects.

When we provide encouragement, we empower another. We can only provide this support, however, when people permit us to look into their minds and hearts. When they do, they show us their souls and allow us to gaze at their dreams. In doing so, they reveal to us the elements of their character. Their beliefs and values go on display. It takes a secure person to exhibit his or her values to another.

Doing so establishes trust and provides a foundation from which we can assess the possibilities for a meaningful relationship. Our need to trust and be trusted is a powerful force. The need to satisfy our relationship's requirement of trust typically has us offering our most intimate secrets as proof of our intent to relate on a higher plane. Once sufficient mental intimacies are exchanged, the bond of trust is established and a relationship of acquaintanceship evolves to one of friendship. Stage one established!

"It takes a lot of courage to show your dreams to someone else."
Erma Bombeck

Fool's Gold
16
Technique

I ntimacies are the currency of trust when attempting to launch a relationship. It is common for two well meaning people to dive headfirst into a physically intimate relationship in an effort to hastily establish a bond of trust. Intimacy can be a mental or physical concept, so it's easy to understand how we sometimes get caught up in relationships that are not at all what we intended them to be. Hollywood constantly promotes sexual intimacy and Madison Avenue reinforces it, so don't be surprised if your brain gets confused and substitutes physical intimacy for mental intimacy as you bond with your new favorite guy.

Be quick to demand from yourself the answer to the question, "Who is this guy and why should I trust him? Are my beliefs and values safe with him? What are *his* beliefs? Would a relationship with him be melodic or just noisy?" If you don't care for his beliefs, you surely won't care for his behavior. That is why it is imperative that your first response must be to discover what's going on inside his head. What does he believe? Is his measuring cup calibrated similarly to yours or is his pint your quart? How low is the cross piece on his goal posts. Is his deep your shallow? What's a fib where he comes from?

There are a number of ways to learn about a person. Unfortunately, the traditional first step called dating can be painful as hell. But then you already knew that. Instead of using dating as the necessary evil first step, why not use it as the heavenly second step? Get answers to key questions about him (see appendices in back for lists and ideas) before you "go out." One of the best ways to do this is the classic meet for coffee or for "caramels." - whatever suits you. Just meet in the daylight for a no pressure, no alcohol chat. What to wear? Go for a casual look to put both of you at ease. Then let the conversation flow. A casual meeting after class at the campus version of Central Perk will usually open your eyes to what you may be in for with this guy and may save you the inconvenience of finding out the hard way… another "seemed like it would never end" date.

Once you get a feel for his character and values you can weigh your interest in him and decide whether to proceed. If you like what you see, hear and feel, and his values appear to align with yours, you may want to begin testing the waters with sensitive issues that are important to you. By engaging him on topics of personal substance early on, instead of waiting, you will accomplish several agendas, not the least of which is postponing the physical agenda until the mental one gets two thumbs up. Whatever comes of your rendezvous, remember – life's too short to fiddle with violins that can't play all the notes you'll need for your concert, so if he's got a string or two missing, pass him up. Better matches are already in the pipeline coming at you. Time will pass and they will just show up. We have a series of compounding strategies that jump the numbers considerably.

If you don't care for his beliefs, you surely won't care for his behavior.

First Goal
17
Strategy

Y our first goal is to learn his beliefs and values, compare them to yours, and answer the question, "Do I really want to go out with this guy?" Sounds simple enough. But exactly how do you go about arranging a time to trade stories and ideas over coffee and reveal a little about this fellow you have your eye on?

Start by saying, "You seem like a pretty interesting guy, Ned. I'd like to get to know you better. Would you like to have coffee some time?" He will not only be impressed with your sense of substance, but will be struck with the realization that he is being shopped. How flattering! Coincidentally, such an evaluation is a very distracting position to be in.

It's going to take some serious thought for both of you to excavate your soul, inventory your thoughts, articulate your values and package the whole thing so that it makes sense for the other's appraisal. That moves sex to the second row in his cranial bleachers. Tension equals laughter, so expect lots of laughs for your first face to face meeting. Once you're there, what then?

Then it's time for the interview. Watch and listen to this guy, up close and personal, for an hour or so. Dancing to a rock band in a dimly lit club is not the stuff that supports idea exchange. But sit and trade stories in a calm environment and you will have some genuine communication on your hands. What does he have to say? What does he want you to hear?

While you both need to communicate your preferences for sights and sounds, art and music, drama and sports, the *character* issues are the real agenda of your casual meeting. Lead with questions that get to the heart of what he believes, and give him the time and space to respond. Shhh – it's revelation time.

Coaches hold tryouts. So should you. If this guy doesn't fit your criteria, you need to know before you put him in uniform. If you wish to pursue him for a relationship, even better, you've already clarified your image of him and learned why dating him is more likely to be a good thing than a regretful one. Too bad you didn't do this with that clown that turned into a total idiot two minutes after getting into his car last semester. This is why it is beneficial to mentally label a guy "prospect" and spend time with him where and when you can walk away from him, without awkwardness and on a moment's notice if need be. Dates, unlike interviews, can be complicated and sometimes nearly impossible to end. The daytime coffee shop scenario makes it easy; you can even give it a time limit in case of emergency. Fire escapes – they're a beautiful thing!

Tension equals laughter,
so expect lots of laughs for your first face to face meeting.

Fire Escape
18
Technique

Set up your meeting for a limited amount of time – say an hour. Create a good excuse to leave at the end of that hour and drop a reminder of it as you sit down. If this is going to turn painful you'll applaud yourself for having prepared a good reason to leave when you said you would. Sometimes even an hour with someone can be too much, however. As an extra precaution you might call your friend as you sit down with him to ask if she's still going to try to color her hair by herself. That's her cue to start the timer. When she calls in 30 minutes …if the guy is obnoxious - you can say that you need to go – your girlfriend is dying her hair and it's going very badly – emergency!

Before you leave do take a moment to pay your half of the check and explain your feelings in a polite way to him. While you think he's an okay guy his ideas differ enough from yours that you wouldn't get along but that there are a lot of girls that *would* find him desirable. Look him in the eyes and smile a sincere smile and tell him you'll keep an eye out for his match.

You've cushioned your personal rejection of him with your feeling of acceptance by lots of others. His reaction will be tempered by the idea that he was treated fairly and not disrespected. When you meet again, as fate will likely have it, you can easily say that you're still keeping an eye out for his match. Be nice and nice things will be your reward.

If, on the other hand, the 30 minutes has been well spent and getting more interesting you can suggest she call another friend who should be arriving soon. In 30 more minutes you can call to see if you can have some extra time before you need to be somewhere thus allowing more than an hour with this guy.

To be able to gracefully extend or curtail the meeting within half hour increments in the first 90 minutes ensures you won't spend more than a half hour of extreme discomfort. Fire escapes: they're a beautiful thing!

Screening
19
Strategy

F un facts like his major or minor, class load, where he lives on or off
campus, favorite hangouts, sports, music, movies, foods and how he
likes his roommate are great ice breakers. However, you should *plan* to
move on to the questions that will reveal core issues sooner than later.
Answers to questions about where he grew up lead to important stuff like
what his family life was like, and the quality of his relationship to his
mother and father, sisters and brothers, will reveal substantial information
about this fellow. It never ceases to amaze me what people will tell you
during a one-on-one conversation, if you just take the time to ask. Take
this exchange, for example:

You: So, growing up on a farm must have been quite an experience. Were
your mom and dad both busy all the time with the farming?

Him: Actually no, my mom ran away with the vacuum cleaner salesman
when I was ten, and our oldest sister raised us until I was in high school.

You: Oh my god! How awful! Did you ever see her again?

Him: Yeah, she's a corporate headhunter in New York. I really *hate her* for
what she did to us and my dad.

You: So did your father ever marry again?

Him: Oh yes - great lady. We all really love her. Her name's Jeri and she's
really a wonderful person.

A simple conversation can provide priceless insight. Recognizing this
person's experiences and traumas may shed light on subsequent behavior.
Crisis weakens some and strengthens others. What did it do to him?
Continue to listen and ask questions as long as you want to listen and he
wants to talk. Order another latte, and watch the human drama unfold. You
may both be witnessing the birth of a splendid new relationship. It's like

unwrapping a present, peeling back the layers of paper and ribbon to reveal what's inside. Use patience, care and respect, and you'll be rewarded with what you learn. What's the stuff that this guy is made of? Do you feel empowered in his presence?

Ask even more questions. What are his thoughts on God and the hereafter? Do questions about U.S. foreign policy draw a blank from him or launch a speech? Ask big questions and find out if he has an opinion. Ask him about his close friends and what draws him to them.. Be on the lookout for values like honesty integrity, courage, work ethic, as well as seemingly less important issues like laziness, punctuality, neatness, cleanliness. You're here to get a preview of your future with this guy. Take what you learn about him and run some "what if scenarios" In your head. Better to lie awake at night dreaming of the possibilities than to spend the "next day" regretting a hasty and irresponsible decision.

"One's philosophy is not best expressed in words; it is expressed in the choices one makes... and the choices we make are ultimately our responsibility." Eleanor Roosevelt

Certain Failure
20
Opportunity

Constant little fibs are more than words – they are behavior. Little fibs equal a big lie and destroy trust, so be sensitive to how he throws around his facts in front of you. An insecure person will inflate reality to cover their lack of perceived stature in your eyes, but liars will tell complete mistruths to manipulate reality. Liars should always be rejected as soon as they are discovered. Where is trust in dishonesty?

> Small stuff becomes a big deal with sufficient repetitions.
> Mighty Oak regarding Gnawing Beaver

Lots of little hurts add up to a big heartache. Don't wait too long before you take off that shoe and shake out the grit causing the irritation. Recognizing trouble in the early stages tends to become easier when we've been there before. Learn from past relationships and refuse to make the same mistake twice. When we catch conflicts at the irritation stage rather than the bleeding stage, we save our emotions for the better things in life.

> "The prompter the refusal, the less the disappointment."
> Publius Syrus

Poorly matched traits can and will eat your relationship for lunch if you're not careful. Recall that roommate from hell your freshman year. Great personality, but left your half of the room looking like her half. Having a slob for a roommate may or may not get on your nerves. Staying at her house one weekend before moving day may have gotten your dorm assignment changed before your semester turned into a jail sentence. But how could a freshman know?

Stop Being a Freshman
21
Strategy

B efore you can secure your destiny with harmony, you need to
continue along the path of discovery. You need to be sensitized to
what in time can make you crazy in a relationship. You know what your
issues are. Doing a more thorough job of sorting out guys typically renders
better results – a lot more often! A solid relationship can then be coached
into a great journey! But you can't have even a short journey with a pebble
in your shoe. The sooner you use this simple yet critical concept, the
quicker you'll come to the right guy. This is one of the most important
ideas you will learn in this book!

If you're with a slightly wrong guy, his presence prevents you from being
with the really right guy. *Slightly* is not the operative word in that sentence;
wrong is. When they're wrong, they're wrong. So just leave it or weep. Not
many "daters" understand this principle. Many women believe it's better to
be in a relationship than not. In fact, many find it embarrassing not to be in
a relationship. They believe it's a sign of failure, unattractiveness or
incompatibility. But whoops, guys typically stay away from women they
perceive as being in relationships. Chances are Mr. Right won't know that
you need rescuing from Mr. Wrong…because you're still with Mr Wrong!
If you wait for your broken relationship to get fixed you may miss out on
meeting a great prospect. Wake up and smell the weeds! How do you tell a
daisy from a dandelion? Keep reading.

p.s. How can you spot a freshman in the rain? They're the ones standing at
the crosswalk - closest to curb… in front of a large puddle. Hmm. Waiting
for their next epiphany shouldn't make you late for class.

Section III

Harmony
Music Theory

First Date
Expectations
Life Plan
Accommodation
Nightclub Eyes
Passion
Practicing Recognition
The Simple Compliment
The Law of Unintended Consequences

"There are two things that people want more than sex and money,
recognition and praise."
Mary Kay Ash, founder Mary Kay Cosmetics

HARMONY

LOVE is the child of harmony.
Harmony comes with accommodation.
Accommodation begins with recognition.
Recognition confers admiration & respect.
Admiration & respect build self confidence.
Self confidence is the engine of accomplishment.
Accomplishment is self actualizing.
Self actualization is fulfillment.
Fulfillment is harmony.
Harmony is bliss.

First Date
22
Technique

L et's presume you've picked one out that feels good, sounds good, and obviously looks good. When you finally suggest it would be fun to go out with him sometime, he may promptly offer to take you to a party, a bar, a movie or maybe even to his place for a video. Be careful; first dates should always begin in public, for safety reasons. So take a walk after a movie downtown, or get a bite to eat at your favorite cafe. Stay away from private, intimate situations until you are further along on your road of discovery. More surprises await you. Play it smart; play it safe.

Finally, finish the latter third or half of the date with another couple – sort of a half of a double date. Notice this technique observes the law of transition. One never leaps completely across a river of unknown depth. One finds a halfway point and lands on that stable rock with one foot until a favorable final landing spot is identified on the other side, and then one completes the crossing with another leap. Leaps of faith are reserved for situations where no alternative exists.

"Don't think there are no crocodiles because the water is calm."
Malayan Proverb

Expectations
23
Opportunity

Y our expectation is for one who can help empower you and you them. How does he take being coached, directed, enabled, and helped? Can he take your advice and not feel put upon, tampered with, manipulated? How do you like advice from him? Some people, it turns out, get along fine until one or the other offers some "help."

Beware. Growing together could be a problem; better catch it early before your endorphins take over and close your eyes to what's best for you. You have to be able to make suggestions and have them thoughtfully evaluated; you cannot be with a person who refuses to consider your ideas meant to benefit them.

If you're not staying intimately aware of his progress by actually coaching and cheering him on, you can't expect to stay connected to him intimately. Once you've lost this mental intimacy, the foundation of your relationship is compromised and you are leaving the door wide open for another to perhaps unwittingly supply it.

The most recurring reason for marriage failure is loss of mental intimacy. Being out of touch with the details of your partner's progress on the critical path to their dreams, the challenges it presents and their efforts to overcome life's everyday obstacles can be fatal to your relationship. Drop the ball, and risk losing the game.

Can he take your advice and not feel put upon, tampered with, manipulated?

Life Plan
24
Strategy

As different as he is from you, you still share an important goal - attaining the highest and best use for the talent and energy each of you brings to the relationship. Agree that your mutual goal with one another is facilitating the other's highest vision of themselves. You will always be critically important to them if you do. Evolving to your potential is known in psychology as self actualization.

We humans never outgrow our need for encouragement, nurturing, enabling, empowerment and interest... which is why it is critical that you have a good coach and cheerleader! Couples who set no long and short term goals for themselves find their relationships wandering aimlessly. Team members need to know the game plan and how they can assist.

> "If one does not know to which port one is sailing,
> no wind is favorable." Seneca

Coach Potatoes Need Not Apply

Aim high, consider yourself capable of great things, move in the direction of your curiosity, and be the best that you can be. Ask yourself what love would do given your talents, energy and resources. Pick someone who will enthusiastically support your efforts to get there! Pick a team player and a great coach, and you'll have a great partner - no, an amazing partner.

We must recognize the full perspective of our relationships. We must cleverly nurture our strengths, our talents and traits, so that we can focus on accommodating them. Should we go to the frat party or surf the net? Hit the mall or take a walk? A close look at the empowering possibilities of each choice is the first priority.

If either person has a talent (a possible career path resource) or trait (a possible character building stimulant) that suggests a priority, let it decide for both of you. Why? Because it matters to that person for reasons sometimes much deeper than you might first suspect. Be sure to communicate why you choose to do one thing over another. As well, ask your date what possible relevance this choice has for him if he really pushes it. You should be getting a better idea of how important recognizing another's "violin strings" are by now if you intend to create harmony and make music with this guy.

Agree that your mutual goal with one another is facilitating
the other's highest vision of themselves.

Accommodation
25
Opportunity

To create this harmony, one must recognize what needs accommodating, recognize what needs empowering. Open the window of respect and be admired and accommodated in return. Then you will experience harmony.

"Love has nothing to do with what you are expecting to get-only with what you are expecting to give - which is everything." Katherine Hepburn

We have already explored the pieces of harmony. The person that accommodates another is usually rewarded by recognition from that person. For example, simply offering him a genuine compliment can swell his heart with pride and increase his feeling of worth as well as yours. Put these principles into daily practice, with people and friends, then feeling good about yourself will become your everyday mood. No more waiting for the weekend!

As your feeling of self worth increases, the courage to express yourself through your wonderful talents will begin to blossom, too. Courage also provides the power to pursue, exercise and discipline those talents. You become motivated to do what you love to do, what you were designed to do, what you are uniquely gifted to do. It's called *doing your thing*! You've now created the engine that will drive you to your personal destination more quickly than anything else.

With courage as your engine and self discipline at the controls, fulfillment becomes the destination, admiration and respect become the scenery, and bliss becomes the traveling companion. Not a bad trip for a gal on her way to a violin concert.

"You'll never do a whole lot unless you're brave enough to try."
Dolly Parton

You must choose a mate whose personality allows you to enable him and as well yourself. Happiness is helping and being helped, caring and being cared for, when the time is right and the need is present. Sometimes we get off track, loose perspective and need to be reminded of our goals. Learning to recognize where a person is in life compared to their stated goals is where you, their coach and cheerleader, come in.

Answering the question, "How can I help this person be happy?" means answering another question first - "How can I accommodate the flower that wants to bloom in the garden of this person's soul? How can I help create harmony for both of us? How can I teach him to create harmony for me?" A key question therefore is: what is this person's grandest dream for themselves and how can I help them identify the next mini-step they need to take and then coach and cheer them to its completion.

Moving steadily along a dream path can be the source of much happiness when someone who cares for you is there to share the grief and share the joy. These people are cherished in return.

"It is one of the beautiful compensations of this life that no one can sincerely try to help another without helping himself."
Charles Dudley Warner

Nightclub Eyes
26
Technique

"See into life, don't just look at it." Anne Baxter

Now we are ready to begin some specially designed calisthenics. These simple mental and verbal exercises will immediately begin building your confidence and self esteem. We're going to give you "nightclub eyes." Intrigued? My experience working in the club and restaurant had me talking with tons of customers, vendors and staff. Early on I became totally bored with the small talk part of the Hospitality business. I don't talk sports or politics so I was motivated to go deeper than small talk for meaningful conversation. It wasn't long before I discovered the power of speaking to people about themselves and specifically about their passions.

Looking into people's personalities for their special talents and character traits I learned the worth of steering the conversation around to their favorite subject - them! I discovered that coaxing perfect strangers (avoid the imperfect* ones) to speak intimately of their favorite personal tales, and recognizing the character traits and talents beneath those stories, makes that person come alive right before your eyes. Everybody has a pride gland just waiting to sponsor a "how cool was that" story about something that rocked their world. Then what? Watch the passion; don't be distracted by the details.

Remember - your goal is not to understand the details of what they're saying, but to recognize the passion revealed in their presentation. Don't worry, the important parts will get through to you. The parts about their repeated failures, persistence, and eventual triumph along with the satisfaction, exhaustion, puzzlement, curiosity, delight, and amazement they encountered along the way will shine right through. You're listening to the music – their passion; don't fret that you can't remember or even understand some of the lyrics!

You may not understand a rodeo but you can relate to the human drama when you see one. You may not understand quantum physics, but you can relate to the human experience when you hear it. You must look to see the passion in the face of the rider; you must listen to hear the drama in the language of the scientist. The experts don't expect you to understand or even repeat back what they are saying. They only want you to enter into their experience and appreciate it. This is a truly intimate moment. Be sure to respect it.

"A man is already halfway in love with any woman who listens to him."
Brendan Francis

Don't ever be afraid to engage anyone in any topic they enjoy talking about. Look for opportunities to ask what excites them about their day, job, hobby, career or major. If they hesitate midway because of the length or depth of the subject, encourage them to continue so that they know it is really them that you are interested in. People will know you are great to talk to when you are an excellent listener. Excellent listeners are rare, always appreciated and highly valued. Be a great listener. It's another power win/win strategy.

Maybe your conversation will go something like this: "So John, what sorts of things are you most into? Like what you're really good at or really serious about – sports, art, science?" Then after listening carefully to his answer, "Oh really? So recall for me a situation where you thought you were going to crash and burn and you somehow turned it around and triumphed in spite of the odds... a time when you were *amazing*." (also in Appendix A)

These seemingly innocuous questions will drill down into a guy's psyche so fast you'll wish you had video taped his reaction for an instant replay. But in case you need to ask again and coax a little to give him time to search his database change the subject, because when he locates his favorite campfire stories you're in for a wild ride. Better yet, you'll get a revealing look at this guy's action machinery. It works on any guy, any age and any relationship. Put it on your key ring. Anytime you need to open a guy up, go for it! Guys love to tell gals about their triumphs as much as gals love looking at little baby's fingers and toes.

*Imperfect strangers: A word to the wise…make contact only with random people who are clearly not in a position to take advantage of you now or later. Recognition can be a very powerful attractant. Heads-up! Use it on guys only after you get to know them as some may mistake it as an invitation.

Passion
27
Technique

L ocate his passion, and get him to tell you his favorite story about it. Can't locate his passion? Tell him one of yours to set his storytelling mind in motion. Suggest you're sitting around a campfire and people are telling jokes and stories, tales about challenges they've had, projects they've undertaken, trips that have gone bad, athletic events that started poorly but turned out great. Situations where extremes challenge a person to deal with the stark reality of success or failure usually unmask the teller. So have several favorite war stories of your own ready for these *just in case situations*.

But what will you learn if not the magic of sub-atomic particles or the "beat-the-clock" precision of pizza delivery? You will learn a variety of amazing things. You will see and hear the enthusiasm of victory or the despair born of defeat. You will begin to gauge the person's confidence and humor or lack thereof. You may even glimpse their honesty and integrity. There's always a surprise inside even if you don't understand the logic or the jargon. The great majority of the time you will relate to the human odyssey - people in search of their limits and sometimes even their dreams!

Whether or not you follow what they are saying, never pass up the opportunity to watch someone come alive. When they realize your lack of basic knowledge for their topic it will be too late, they will already admire your patient focus and take it as a great compliment that you suffered through so much to listen to *them*. You can't lose. Watch how they turn to learn all about this fascinating person (you), who admires them so much as to tolerate a whole harangue about a subject that you may know absolutely nothing about! Let them discover you are a person who loves the human drama and couldn't pass up a demonstration of their passion. You will strike them as a remarkable, even wise, person.

Traits are the facets on the diamond called personality. Honesty, integrity, courage, humor, sensitivity, sincerity, curiosity, and dependability are a few that come to mind. Like a jeweler's apprentice learns to familiarize them self with the features of precious stones, you must become familiar with the facets of personalities. You are planning to make a major investment when you align yourself for life with a man. If you expect to play music with this violin you will have to listen with an educated ear to the sounds it makes in response to your tweaking and plucking. "Educated" presumes preparation *before* examination. You need to acquire the skill before its time to use it.

"Everyday I'm building a fire. And everyday I train and add more fuel. And at just the right moment I light the match."
Mia Hamm

Practicing Recognition
28
Technique

N ow you know that the first step is to develop your listening skills. The second step is to develop your recognition skills. It's in this second step that things really get exciting as you actually activate the harmonic chain reaction. You point out someone's positive trait, you identify why it makes you feel good, and you compliment them on it.

They feel good, you feel good; their confidence increases, so does yours. It's simple stuff, really... like smiling at an elderly woman at the bus stop. Doesn't cost you anything but has great value to the recipient. It warms both your hearts. This is not brain surgery, but heart therapy for sure.

Everything you say and do is for real. The people you encounter are real, so your admiring and complimenting a quality in them should be sincere. Yes, you have a hidden agenda, but it is entirely beneficial, a win-win. You have a long range plan that has both short term and long term benefits to a number of people.

You are attempting to better yourself by bettering the people around you. You are a welcome addition in the garden of pedestrians you will meet along life's path. You are practicing a life skill you will use to identify, grow and maintain the vitality of those you are close to, and especially the dearest one. You'll even give him a green thumb in the process!

You point out someone's positive trait, you identify why it makes you feel good, and you compliment them on it.

The Simple Compliment
29
Technique

When you tweak someone's "strings," you'll feel it and hear it. But you're just getting warmed up! Keep practicing on acquaintances until your delivery becomes smooth. Now set your sights on someone closer, maybe that messy roommate of yours or some other friend who won't mind your mischief. After sufficient practice, your focus will begin to sharpen and you'll start to peer below the surface of more distant people, seeing good and bad. Set aside the bad! Note the good.

Identify a unique trait, a nice one. Why do you like it? How does it affect you? Learn to measure your feelings, and begin consciously valuing people for their good and telling them about it. People will appreciate the good words and begin to view you in a more positive light. Make sure to keep simple compliments light and airy and go easy on the drama. After all, cute freckles are only just that.

"The giving of love is an education in itself." Eleanor Roosevelt

Now for the big action - aim for a genuine, noble trait. Plan the moment well… a casual, "just in passing" notion. Like using a bow and arrow, it's not necessary to draw the compliment way back before letting it go; the slightest inference will sail it to the mark. Admiration and respect will surely follow. So practice your archery, exercise those recognition muscles, and when the time is right, watch Cupid work his magic.

"Do not go where the path may lead; go instead where there is no path and leave a trail." Ralph Waldo Emerson

Needless to say, you're well on your way to wreaking certain havoc in other's insecurities, depression, and bad attitudes as your sunshine starts to blast non-accommodating behavior from your path. The sweet smell of harmony seems to be in the air!

The Law of Unintended Consequences
30
Opportunity

P eople absolutely thrive on robust, positive attitudes. You will be a
source of sunshine; maybe the only source for some! Think about that
- sad but true. Your life has now expanded to include "salt of the earth."
You're adding flavor to lives that have perhaps become dull and flavorless.
Some very powerful stuff is happening now! Better fasten your cloud-belt
because that's where you'll be riding as you witness the wonderful surprise
turns your life will begin to make along the way.

"There is no greater invitation to love than loving first."
St. Augustine

Now for the good stuff. Guys can spot sunshine in a woman in the middle
of a tied ball game, from beneath the hood of an exotic car, even while
wolfing down a double cheese pizza. When you began sharing your casual
admiration with people you began changing your attitude as well. When
you make others feel better about themselves, you begin to feel better about
yourself, too. Feeling better is part of an overall attitude change that will
positively affect everything that you do. Your attitude is experiencing a
make-over and your attractiveness is increasing as a direct result.

"If you think a complimentary thought about someone, don't just think it.
Dare to compliment people and pass on compliments to them from others."
Catherine Ponder

Expand this positive activity to include frequent eye contact, smiling,
holding doors, and offering others a seat on the bus around campus. People
stop being distant and start acting like acquaintances.

People smile back returning your "Hi" and thank you with their eyes. The
recognition you get from these new "friends" fuels your positive attitude.
Happiness is no longer a future goal; it's an everyday presence. It's no longer
something that waits for the weekend.

It's something that's spontaneously happening all around you everyday. Welcome to happiness. It *is* a real place, Toto.

Other people's warmth and kindness is always just below the surface waiting to be released by your first effort. You will not believe how thin that veil is. People create a cold surface as much by their absence of thought as they do by purposely wanting to appear distant. In either case a little recognition, usually a smile or a wink, will melt the moment.

You will be surprised at how positive energy will seek you out, surround you, comfort and insulate you from life's bad luck. *Solutions will begin beating problems to your door.* You'll think your guardian angel finally discovered your hiding place and is trying desperately to make up for lost time. You'll quickly find out that I'm not exaggerating. Most college students, for instance, count themselves lucky to have a geek on the floor or next door for those surprise computer disasters. You'll begin to understand my point when these people just start showing up *before* the crisis. In fact, you will regularly begin receiving solutions to all sorts of predicaments before the problems even arise.

Your attitude is experiencing a make-over and your attractiveness is increasing as a direct result.

"Love makes your soul crawl out from its hiding place."
Zora Neale Hurston

Section IV

The Master Plan
"Instruction"

Your Secret Admirers
Picture Your Dream
The Sincere Compliment
Spontaneous Appearances
Opportunity Thinking
The Conversation
Making Magic
Signatures
Touching
Sarcasm
Best Technique Ever
Preventive Maintenance
Ego Maintenance
Role Validation
The Manly Image
Whisper Power

HARMONY

LOVE is the child of harmony.
Harmony comes with accommodation.
Accommodation begins with recognition.
Recognition confers admiration & respect.
Admiration & respect build self confidence.
Self confidence is the engine of accomplishment.
Accomplishment is self actualizing.
Self actualization is fulfillment.
Fulfillment is harmony.
Harmony is bliss.

Your Secret Admirers
31
Opportunity

M ore good news: Every moment of every day the guys have got their eyes tuned to *their* Discovery Channel. So what happens when Miss Positive Attitude surfs into view - YOU get discovered... at the 7/11, the Laundromat, the library counter, dorm foyer...hey everywhere you choose to recognize your fellow planet dwellers: students, pedestrians, teachers - everyone that gives you an opportunity to accommodate them, becomes your target: over-weight, tall, short or skinny; young or old, black or white, ugly, mean or lean: here you come, ready to hold a door, move a chair, grant a smile and provoke a stare. Oh, and those delightful, *thoughtful* compliments.

The more secret admirers you prepare, the better your odds become in meeting positive attitude guys. You're taking an active role in your own discovery by maximizing your attractiveness - the right kind! The kind that doesn't frizz up when it rains, smear when it's humid, or run when you perspire. You always look great to him. So many angels are just too much for him. Need I remind you...

Cupid is an angel.

Picture Your Dream
32
Opportunity

Y ou've no doubt experienced people with this kind of positive energy. They are a sight for sore eyes. Their wonderment makes them immediately attractive whether or not their hair or makeup looks great. How did they get this way? Some might be born with a sunny disposition. Others see a picture of what they want and through trial and error, study and practice, learn to limp, walk, skip, and finally, run!

The key is to picture your dream in your mind's eye. Get a mental picture of what you want to be. Begin to actively create the details, and sense your unconscious mind start configuring ways to accomplish it. Like a sort of secret shopper in your head, you begin spotting opportunities. Imagine yourself helping people, being extra nice to people, lending a hand - simple, common, thoughtful little things – and that is the person you will become.

"Fear makes strangers of people who would be friends."　Shirley MacLaine

Stop for a second and think about the possibilities of one afternoon. When you use your eyes and ears to spot another's need, you'll find endless opportunities. You may sense the chance to say "I see you" with a smile to a passing stranger; to let someone know after class that their opinion on a topic was cleverly stated; to tell a mentally challenged server in the dining hall that you appreciate the special care they take everyday; to tell a clerk something more than "thanks a lot." These are kind gestures that will not go unnoticed.

Begin to actively create the details, and sense your unconscious mind start configuring ways to accomplish it.

The Sincere Compliment
33
Technique

W hen you look at a friend or stranger, look closely. Find positive traits or talents that shine and voice them when the opportunity presents itself. Take your time, quality counts. Sometimes time is short. Take a minute then to rehearse the points you want to make. Speak the words in your mind. Hear the words.

"It took a lot of courage to *dispute* that theory with the prof. I really admire your special talent for *diplomacy*. Few students could have pulled it off as well as you."

Hmm – dispute and diplomacy were really a great fit. They allowed you to say it all with few words without sounding gushy. You have the vocabulary. Take a minute to let your brain "look it up."   Or, how about this?

"Wow! Wanda was *really* upset about the grade she got on that Lit paper; it's too bad she had to take it out on you. I was impressed at how you just *absorbed* the whole thing. Your patience is a special gift."

Okay, absorb was a little weird – but you made your point and the point was that she deserved a pat on the back and you were there for her. Now repeat the word absorb with some drama and you can both share a laugh about your homely choice of words. You ain't perfect but you're more better than you used to got!

✿   Tell 'em what they did.
✿   Tell 'em how it made you feel.
✿   Verbalize their special trait or talent. (Text messaging works.)

"The best and most beautiful things in the world cannot be seen or even touched - they must be felt with the heart." Helen Keller

Spontaneous Appearances
34
Opportunity

O kay, you've got a new goal – *a new you*, one whose sun shines for everyone. The next question becomes how to deal with the guys that the new you begins to attract. They'll begin coming out of the woodwork to accommodate *you* now. They've seen and studied your behavior, and now they're waiting for the opportunity to meet you. Meeting you is easier than meeting the average woman because you're open and friendly to everyone, and they noticed.

Being friendly not only makes it easier for "regular" guys to introduce themselves, but it also expands the field of guys to include the shy ones. Your behavior is actually empowering men and you haven't even met one yet! It's like spontaneous combustion, only with men

"Very often the only way to get a quality in reality is to
start behaving as if you already had it."
C.S. Lewis

Opportunity Thinking
35
Strategy

Y ou now have some of the critical ingredients for finding, winning, and holding onto that very special guy. Let's proceed then to the strategy for making music with him. I had you pick up your bow and begin fiddling around on other people's strings to familiarize you with creating pleasant sounding notes. Once you acquired a natural feel for it, I asked that you pick up the pace and begin fiddling around everywhere you went. You began surrounding yourself with the music that recognition triggers.

"And the day came when the risk to remain tight in a bud was more painful than the risk it took to blossom." Anais Nin

Watching for opportunities to supply other's minor needs as well as recognizing their character strengths has become a vehicle now *for your own empowerment.* Your personality begins to react as your body would to exercise and nutrition. It glows with vitality. An exercised, healthy, vital body easily meets the challenges of stress and exertion.

A heart filled with the joy of sharing simple love, the kind you exercise just in passing, easily absorbs the slights and minor put-downs that life inadvertently brings. So it follows that your personality will now respond more positively to the stress and exertion of interacting with any special man you come across.

"You gain strength, courage, and confidence by every experience in which you really stop to look fear in the face. You are able to say to yourself, 'I have lived through this horror. I can take the next thing that comes along.' You must do the thing you think you cannot do." Eleanor Roosevelt

I don't have to tell you just how stressful confronting a person that you are profoundly attracted to can be. Our muscles tense, our body chemistry changes and our brains rev-up to perform multiple, simultaneous calculations at lightning speed. Meeting a special person initiates a litany of questions.

"How do I look and sound to this person? Does he sense my tension? How could I possibly have said what I just did? Am I even making sense to him right now? What must he think of me?

Guess what? A similar storm is raging in his head, too, but he looks so together and your hair is such a mess and what if this and that...Stop right there. This is the girl you used to be; not the woman you've become. The practice you've religiously performed stands fortified to defend you. You are now an accomplished impromptu speaker with several tricks up your sleeve.

At the drop of a hat you can deflect attention away from yourself and turn the conversation to recognize another's qualities. Now, with a semester of practice, you are equipped to deflect the conversation away from yourself and turn it entirely to this new fellow. It will send his ego into a pleasant state of euphoria as he recounts some favorite life event. You have achieved a second degree, black belt in social martial arts!

"We don't know who we are until we see what we can do."
Martha Grimes

The Conversation
36
Technique

You've learned to repeat the speaker's sentences in a fashion that begs their elaboration. You are well practiced at appearing wise by saying little. You can easily disarm an attacker with a personal compliment at a moment's notice. Once you make it a regular habit to offer simple compliments in light conversations with people you know and don't know, you are prepared to pick up a fiddle, step up on stage and play a little duet with any musician anytime. Such is the power of practice - lots of continuous practice.

Once you make-over your perspective and reorient your focus from "What's happenin?" to "Let me tell you something cool I noticed about you today!" you will be in charge of what goes on in your head when these spontaneous moments explode in your life. Let's just take a leap here and say a prospect comes into your sights, somebody you would consider going out with. Maybe you have been scoping a guy at the Union for some time. He's in the food court, seated at the table beside you. You notice a textbook by his plate that suggests engineering. You've been practicing the last few weeks on people, so you're ready... if you can just think of something to say about engineering.

You: "Hi, excuse me, I couldn't help but notice your engineering book."

Him: "Huh? Oh, sorry. Didn't realize you were speaking to me. I was just wondering how I can get my bike out of a tree behind our apartment. I live with some guys that consider themselves clever to a point of inconvenience sometimes. I'm sorry, what were you saying?"

(You decide to set aside the obvious conversation about his clever friends and stay with your original plan, *him*.)

You: "I take it that by your books there that you are an engineering major."

Him: "Yes, actually the mechanical kind." He grins.

You: "You must have quite a memory, with all those formulas and stuff. Were you able to memorize things easily all your life?"

Him: "Ah, not really. I mean, stuff like poems and dates in history I'm really pretty bad with, but my mom used to really get on me to study my homework. So I usually got it, but it took a lot of work."

You: "Is your mother a literary type, an artist... or a scientific type like you appear to be? By the way, you seem very poised, self confident." (He doesn't, but you're going to drop a hot one on him to take a quick peek inside "his violin case" - might be a major string there you can play.)

Him: "Whoa, you really think so? Actually, I'm quite nervous. I mean not because of you, but just generally around people I first meet."

You: "Wow, it's not often a guy will admit to being nervous. It's nice to meet someone who isn't scared to be honest. Hey, I've actually got to run. I'm sure I'll see you around." And with a grin, "Maybe next time you can tell me how the bike in the tree story turns out."

Him: "Sure, you bet. I'll tell you all about it." He waves as you get up.

If you need to kill some time while you eat ask him about the best prank he's ever pulled. Wow, now you're going to hear passion and drama in a short story that will speak volumes!

The Critique

That little scene just generated something that you both will look forward to. Best of all, he knows that he feels good about himself when the two of you are together. You could have sat there and missed your next class with this guy, but did you really want that first meeting to go longer than a few minutes? By controlling the scene, you prevented it from becoming more than either one of you could process. It's best to leave at a high point, his endorphins raging and you making a great first impression. Now if you can just calm those butterflies in your stomach.

Making Magic
37
Opportunity

R ecognition can mean two things: spotting a trait worth commenting on and/or awarding praise. For instance, you might say to a senior citizen in the supermarket parking lot, "Letting that busy clerk know back there that she gave you an extra ten dollars in change was impressive! It's nice to see honest people speak up. You get a good citizen award for that." Now, instead of just mouthing the words sincerely, add a little passion to your voice and body language, like Elaine on Seinfeld and you've got something twice as good! You just made it fun for both of you and still supplied admiration and respect, and the other person thinks you're the cool gal of the day for expressing it with some pizzazz.

There's a little blurb in the Bible that refers to being "the light of the world and the salt of the earth." I think it means illuminating goodness where and when you find it - like someone's special moment - then sprinkling it with some recognition to enhance the experience. Capturing special moments is powerful stuff! Picture yourself with a flashlight in one pocket and a handful of applause in the other, ready to help others stop and smell the roses along life's sometimes dreary path.

Imagine hundreds of thousands of people behaving in this positive way. Do you believe that some behaviors can get a life of their own and begin multiplying themselves? When you remember that acts as these trigger natural opiates, it is easy to understand why. There are personalities out here in search of a model. Would you consider yourself worthy of influencing another's behavior for the benefit of all? Do you believe that what goes around comes around? Maybe it's time to believe in a little magic.

"Never believe that a few caring people can't change the world. For, indeed, that's all who ever have." Margaret Mead

Signatures
38
Strategy

A champion of the emotionally starved is the person who can project mental images of their happiest moments. You're not using videotape or even digital technology. You're retelling *his* favorite "war stories," the moments of triumph, big and little, where his unique character and passion for the moment wowed you and anyone else that may have been watching. These are the helping, caring, sharing, empowering moments that made him tall in your eyes; those struggles with adversity saw him rise to the challenge and excel. It is this image that inspires you. Why, you simply cannot imagine hitching your wagon to any other star than his!

A compelling reason for looking deep into a person's character and seeing his unique and special gifts of personality is the ability to recognize the signature in his behavior. If you've watched carefully, you'll catch lots of glimpses of his greatness. If you're wise, you'll collect them in your mental scrapbook; there's no telling when you'll need to review them with him. It's important to note some details about the moments that shine.

"We deceive ourselves when we fancy that only weakness needs support. Strength needs it far more." Madame Swetchine

If you can't be each other's biggest fans - jumping up in the stands at those big moments, cheering each other on to victory - then just how do you two expect to achieve victory? Imagine a team playing without a cheering section. Now, even worse, imagine a team without a coach. Are you starting to get the picture? You two need to make a team effort - two players, two coaches, two cheerleaders. One strategy - three roles. Are you starting to see how one gets game?

Touching
39
Technique

A nytime you'd like to be heard, just touch someone first. Ever notice how when two moms are talking at the market, the kid wanting attention touches his mother when words won't do the trick? I used the technique while teaching eighth graders. For years I got their attention by walking down the aisle and lightly putting my hand on their shoulder while reiterating a statement to someone who obviously was in another world. More often than not, they could repeat verbatim what I had just said; and sometimes even quote me the following week.

Let's Get Physical

Touching even worked on trouble makers at the bar. As soon as I spotted mischief makers, I would approach them with a big smile, appear oblivious to the mischief, introduce myself, shake hands with everyone, ask them where they were from, and tell them how happy I was that they had picked my club to party at. Then I would put my hand on the chief mischief maker's shoulder or arm and tell him or her that if they needed anything I would be personally happy to get it for them.

That was usually the end of it as they had just unwittingly received the excitement their mischief had initially been designed to attract – a close call with the owner of the club. I always made a point of checking back with them to let them know I hadn't forgotten them. I also made it a point to give them my business card with a glossy color picture of the club on the front and a hand written, free cover message for the doorman on the back for their next visit.

Recognition is enhanced by physical touch. Instead of filling the club with troublemakers, I filled it with people who returned for their recognition fix. My policy was to catch them doing positive stuff as well. These ex-mischief-makers became "regulars" who looked out for the rest of us when our backs were turned. They became ambassadors, convincing others that we were the good guys and fooling around was not cool "in their bar." Recognition – it works like magic.

Electricity for Effect

So what do you do to make a thought really stick in his head? Three major factors combine to create an effect greater than their sum would suggest. Let's look at this powerful formula and analyze its effects.

- ❖ You caught him doing something positive.
- ❖ You confronted him with it immediately.
- ❖ You touched him.

Touching is a powerful, seldom employed communication resource which helps emphasize the effect. Touching can have a startling effect on people. The key is the element of surprise. When we are surprised numerous defense mechanisms are immediately deployed. The pulse quickens, blood pressure increases, and our perceptions amp all the way up. Our brain begins processing quicker and the event seems to unfold slower so that incoming data can be processed more thoroughly and be better understood. To say that your target became very attentive and acutely focused would be accurate.

To say that you created an event that was least likely to be forgotten would be true. In fact, you created a powerful event that will deeply embed its message by linking three emotionally charged cues together because each of the five perceptions has its own filing system in the mind. A new folder was added not to just the "heard" file. Folders were also opened in the "felt" and "seen" files as well. This became a three dimensional memory. How clever of you. To say the episode was *memorable* would be accurate. Goal achieved!

Recognition, use lots of folders – it works like magic.

Sarcasm
40
Opportunity

G uys like being coached. Since clear communication is crucial to sending your thoughts to others, refrain from sending clouded, coded, complex signals. Being cool comes second to being clearly understood. So avoid being sarcastic and teach him not to be. By speaking in an overly dramatic way and saying the opposite of what you mean, your attempt to be clever and humorous can deliver mixed signals. It's tough enough that we have to encode our thoughts into sounds that must be heard and interpreted by others. Why run the risk of miscommunication by reversing meanings, when the other person is also trying to sense your emotions and interpret your body language, too. Often the first thing we say is taken as gospel. It's important to release the true, sincere message first.

> "Sarcasm is the language of the devil, for which reason
> I have long since renounced it." Thomas Carlyle

Intimacy Snub - unintended

Sarcasm jerks around the recipient by sending the *opposite* of the true message, then, does a quick reverse to release the tension.

Bob: "So Ginny, did you see the note I slipped into your lab book at lunch?"

Ginny: "No, I was too busy memorizing the periodic tables for a pop quiz. I put it under a leaky bottle of sulfuric acid ... It kind of melted away, was it something important?" Then after an awkward pause, "Yea, I saw it." She continues grinning, "It fell out when I opened it up. That was really sweet of you to surprise me."

That's an ill chosen, expensive joke. He'll think twice about expressing his intimate feelings to you in the future since you'd rather make fun of them than be assured by them. Sarcasm has more pitfalls than applause potential, so it's best to leave it alone. His buddies may like it, but you're not the entertainment here. You're the messenger attempting a grand experiment in harmony and love. Be fun, be humorous, but be sincere. He'll really like the fact that you're easy to understand. Be funny later, but first deliver the true answer with sincerity.

Ginny, take two: "Yea, it made my day to find your note. You're the greatest!" (Big hug) "I felt like the luckiest girl on campus to have such a sweet guy."

Being cool comes second to being clearly understood.

Best Technique Ever
41
Opportunity

"What men and women need is encouragement...Instead of always harping on a man's faults, tell him of his virtues. Try to pull him out of his rut of bad habits." Eleanor H Porter

Once while flipping through a restaurant magazine, I came across the mantra of a wise old football coach – "Catch 'em doing something right, anything really - no matter how small - especially if the person is an underachiever... and ignore everything else." Eliminate not only negative criticism, but the appearance of criticism of any sort.

The idea was to ignore what the players did wrong and compliment them on what they did right. During coaching sessions the players would see and hear what was right and wrong *as a group*. If references were made to anyone in particular, it would be only in the positive. If a player was observed doing something right in practice or at a game, he was immediately complimented on it. He was to be told specifically what was observed and how it made the coach feel.

For example, if the coach observes a football player blocking the opposing player with his arms too low, communicating it appropriately doesn't sound like this: (Yelling loud enough for the ladies on the lacrosse field to hear) "Hey Conrad, you bozo! Don't put your arms down around your belt buckle when you hit somebody! Get 'em up high, like in his chest!"

Instead, effective communication is framed in the context of what the player should have done right, like this: (Grinning widely) "Nice going, Conrad. You make music in my head when I see how you come off your knuckles quickly like that at the snap, keeping your arms chest-high with a nice follow-through to drive him off to the side ... reminds me of some of my finest moments at State." The coach puts his arms up mimicking the correct arm position as if Conrad had actually done that. He nods an affirmative, then pats the player on the shoulder and walks back to the sidelines.

Interesting… somewhere in that compliment he snuck in his message, and the player runs back onto the field encouraged with his new self image "cut and pasted" right over the reality as if it had never occurred. Nice behavior editing, eh?

"Whoa," I remember thinking, "sounds like these coaches have found the holy grail of *behavior modification*." The article went on to explain that experiencing the thrill of being caught at something done right gives the players an exaggerated boost because they were expecting to be criticized when in fact they were complimented. The result is that they immediately launch into behavior designed to getting caught again. They really get addicted to this spontaneous praise and recognition. Sound familiar?

> "Our chief want in life is someone who will make us do what we can.
> Ralph Waldo Emerson

People get a thrill out of being caught in the act of doing something right for a change. If the "catcher" bothers to figure out what positive trait or talent is being demonstrated by the act and points that out too, then the harmonic effect becomes a very valuable learning tool. If the catcher touches the other person while pointing out the trait or talent, the thought goes platinum. If the two have a relationship that is already based on mutual admiration, then the impact of the reaction is hard to measure without a seismograph!

> "Friendship is a strong and habitual inclination in two persons to promote the good and happiness of one another."
> Eustace Budgell

Preventive Maintenance
42
Strategy

The recommended method for preventing breakdowns and ensuring peak performance is called PM - that's preventive maintenance for you non-engineering students. Rather than make repairs *after* his self image has worn thin, his service manual recommends frequent lubrication of the behavior modulator that lets positive character traits shine through. What does this mean? Well, our day is filled with behavior that attempts to translate our thoughts into meaningful results.

Our mood has a lot to do with whether we proceed this week, this day, or this hour along our dream path or elect to just be complacent about opportunities and be ornery with everyone that crosses our path. With lots of positive thoughts, we become our best selves and extend our reach to brighten other people's day. In a depressed temperament we become insecure and adopt the lobster's approach, take on a hardened exterior and drag around on the bottom doing not much else. Somebody gets in our face they get their choice of pincers!

The value derived from recognition, especially the variety we are exploring here, has the power of the universe within it. Love comes from harmony; harmony comes from accommodation; and recognition is usually the best place to start the chain reaction - especially before emotional emergencies arise. If your grades are better than his, if it appears you will be making more money than he will, if you are physically near his equal in strength or size, or you're just hitting the ball a lot better than he is; you may have a bit of recognition work to do.

Remember, quality counts! A healthy self esteem is your best ally when his feelings start sending up error messages about your future with him. Toasters flying around the kitchen is usually a pretty good signal that his self esteem is bouncing on empty. You may want to review his "image tapes" for the last ten days. Oh, and you may want to check the dates on your receipts for recent "ego fill-ups." You *are* mentally taping everything he seems to feel is an event in his life as he reports it, aren't you? Squeaky gears need oil before they overheat.

Since guys are not taught to feel but to calculate, he may not be able to self assess. Adding up why he feels the way he does may not produce an answer for him. He just feels down! You may have to use your powers of feeling to figure it out. Lucky thing he's got you, huh?

Tidbits of recognition are a sure-fire daily vitamin regimen for healthy self esteem and a quick mega dose is indicated anytime stress is observed. Public knowledge of our triumphs and defeats always exaggerates the impact to our pride. As your guy's mental health EMT (emotional medical technician) you should be prepared to stop a hemorrhage in the pride reservoir or splint a fractured image immediately. Keeping a mental file of your guy's big moments and best war stories as well as a quick list of his character strengths means having a well stocked first aid kit to draw from once the patient is stabilized and able to listen.

A freaked-out psyche is better treated with a listening ear than a pep talk. Once his blood pressure (pronounced veins on his forehead, artery on neck, reddish color face) returns to normal and he's all talked out about whatever it was that derailed his train, the motivational therapy can begin. Remember, warriors make bad listeners; so if he's still in kill mode you need to be patient, nod your head a lot and sit through it. Oh, and move the lamp and hide the toaster.

"All the affectionate feelings of one for others are extensions of one's feelings for oneself." Aristotle

Ego Maintenance
43
Technique

Y our daily vitamins in his ear as well as timely first aid can go a long way to maintaining an ego that pulls it's own weight in your relationship. "High-fiving" spontaneous signature moments replayed for the courage-building they generate is the daily regimen for confident, believe-in-myself, follow-my-dream thinking.

Catching each other in signature moments, the times when we truly demonstrate the sweet essence of our character or talent, is Job One for both partners. These are the moments that generate the energy that drives the engine of accomplishment along its critical path to its greatest good, its grandest dream. So collecting these moments, these tidbits of behavior, and storing them in a jar near the front of your head, dispensing them daily to remind yourselves just how great your uniqueness is and how much you are appreciated for just being yourselves, should be considered your top priority.

Act as each other's trophy case, housing every blue ribbon moment whether gained at the deli or at class, in the lab or on the Union, ping pong table, or waiting in line for a movie. Applaud it, mentally record it and then reiterate it. Quality shareware – no copyright. Rip every one.

"There is nothing better than the encouragement of a good friend."
Katherine Hathaway

Role Validation
44
Technique

How does he know thee? Let us count the ways. But first ask yourself, "How do I wish to be known: as a lover, a friend, a coach and a partner?" Or perhaps more importantly, "How do I wish *not* to be known: as a maid, a mother, and a boss?" If you are not careful, it's easy to send these signals and mislabel yourself permanently, when you raise your voice and order him around. Now that you are mindful of how you condition your image in his mind, it would be wise to consider your actions and motives carefully. Don't pick up after him, unless the maid image works for you. Threatening him with physical violence changes your image to warrior and, of course, you don't ever want to go there. Be a nurturer, a coach, a confidant, a lover and a partner and you'll likely be treated as such.

Pointing out negative behavior does not positively affect behavior, which is why the coaches did not bother trying to make a player *unlearn* something. Better to learn something new right over the top of the old. Remember those boys in grade school? The only effective way to get them to change their behavior was by adding recess (playground), not taking it away. The thought of more recess time playing conditioned their mind to *eagerly hear* what was being said and place it in a positive light. It motivated them to adopt whatever behavior it took to realize the goal, recess, even if that meant shutting up and not showing off for a whole class period.

Take the old fashioned custom of opening doors for you, standing up when you enter the room, helping you with your chair, or carrying out your trash. Most guys never focus much on this stuff. But tell him that *it makes you feel like a lady* when he does, he'll be racking his brain for similar opportunities to duplicate your response. Your feeling like a lady suggests he's acting like a man. Since he loves feeling like a man in your eyes, he only has to perform the acts that trigger your lady-like feelings. You get to name what they are! A nice little discovery, huh? Worth the price of the book as they say on the carnival midway.

The Manly Image
45
Technique

He craves to know what makes you feel like a lady so that his manly nature can be exercised, recognized and appreciated. Make sure you catch him doing these right things frequently and *ignoring* his slips, - no grimacing allowed - until the habit sets like cement. Then tell him every few days *how much like a lady* he makes you feel. Like a Google search, his mind will race to every behavior you've affectionately associated with these ladylike feelings and every past suggestion will be updated automatically.

Everyone admires those who appreciate them for the little things they do. He'll feel great about all those things that up to meeting you were just thankless, pesky little tasks people barked at him about. Wow, somebody to appreciate him for his goodness, instead of cute, smart, rich or tall – which were not his choice. That will make you *his* someone special. Is that what you wanted? As the outdoorsmen like to say, "This dog wants to hunt!"

Your affectionate, dramatic, little mentions about how his putting down the lid, taking out the trash, picking up his stuff, standing-up when you enter the room, unlocking your side of the car first are the treats that propels this dog to hunt and feel good about himself and his performance. They feed the relationship mega-vitamins in bite-sized, concentrated doses. Don't miss any opportunity to amp-up your reaction to his positive behavior.

Make a point of over-dramatizing by adding facial expression, body language, smile, wink, touch and you'll feel like you just invented Crazy Glue. This stuff really makes it stick! A few more tools and you'll be dangerous. If ever you needed to be a drama queen this is it! Too much drama like too much ice cream and cake at a birthday party is not a problem. He's got a bigggg freezer! He'll dole it out as his hunger requires. It's your job to keep it well stocked. Drama: it's a beautiful thing.

"I hear and I forget. I see and I remember. I do and I understand."
Confucius

Whisper Power
46
Opportunity

"For it was not into my ear you whispered, but into my heart. It was not my lips you kissed, but my soul." Judy Garland

Deliver these messages in a whisper, and you've added fuel to the fire of change. Lowering your voice to the tone and volume used for affection and intimacy creates a special environment, a mating environment. The mating environment carries its own powerful opiates, and so the leverage you've achieved by using this extraordinary paradigm on top of the synergies you've already incorporated into your strategy are nothing less than heaven sent. In fact, that's exactly what they are. You are engaged in the grandest of all earthly expeditions, traveling to the land of harmony and love, to your dreams and his. You're certainly welcome to employ all the wonderful resources your nature makes available, no matter how unglamorous the message. Even little irritations will conflict us as long as we don't deal with them – like his refusal to put down the lid. Consider that mailing a priority message is best shipped with special packaging to alert the handlers to its special contents. A special delivery package makes any message priority and special. Clever you. This message from your local post office.

Physically it looks like you:
- ❖ Create suspense by acting like you're catching him at something.
- ❖ Approach him and lower your voice to a whisper.
- ❖ Compliment him on some ideal activity.
- ❖ Tell him that it makes you feel, "like a lady."
- ❖ Hug him.

What really happened? You:

- ❖ Acquired his undivided attention.
- ❖ Released natural opiates.
- ❖ Pasted in a new behavior.
- ❖ Released natural opiates (again!).
- ❖ Electrified his nervous system and bonded the thought.

Now you have accomplished behavior modification, and reordered his priorities to align with yours. You turned a negative situation into a warm, intimate little scene that shared affection with communication. If you are extra quiet while expressing yourself to him, you have added the feature of intimacy.

Now don't despair thinking this is just too simple to work or that it is too much maintenance to do. Once he's oriented to your style of support for him, he'll fall right into a comfort zone that will take very little effort to maintain and as well reciprocate. Can you deal with your ego *and* his? Remember the way the flowers bend in the direction of the sunshine? Your guy will react identically! Shooting his heart full of recognition arrows will never fail to maintain his admiration and respect for you. In a while I'll show you how to teach him to return the favor to *you.* This thing doesn't work unless both dancers move their feet.

You turned a negative situation into a warm, intimate little scene that
shared affection with communication.

"Leadership is the art of getting someone else to do something you want
done because he wants to do it."
Dwight D. Eisenhower

Section V

The Date
The Recital

Try-Out Dating
Try-Out Date
Looking Hot
Double Dates
Offbeat Tunes
The Jerk
The Dishonor Maneuver
Physical Distractions
Charisma
Recycle 'Em
Exit Science
Predictability
Pleading Temporary Infatuation
Character & Virtue
Assembling Composite
Critique Him
Subtle Echo

HARMONY

LOVE is the child of harmony.
Harmony comes with accommodation.
Accommodation begins with recognition.
Recognition confers admiration & respect.
Admiration & respect build self confidence.
Self confidence is the engine of accomplishment.
Accomplishment is self actualizing.
Self actualization is fulfillment.
Fulfillment is harmony.
Harmony is bliss.

Try-Out Dating
47
Opportunity

Y our sunshine has attracted someone's interest and you've casually
"interviewed" each other. Your questions have gone deep into the core
of your personalities. From this interviewing process, a couple of two hour
afternoon coffees downtown or at the Union, you've concluded you share
the same beliefs and values. Beliefs and values do not mean artistic tastes like
musical groups, dance clubs, or favorite junk food. So you've agreed to give
him a shot, decided to take a chance, and go out on a date. Absolutely,
positively... keep it simple.

A deluge of feelings will challenge your sanity. Keep it simple. Your brain is
the only thing that stands between you and miscalculating him. Want a
recipe for disaster? Dress to kill, have too many cocktails, give mixed
messages, and wake up the next day dazed and confused. Your heart will
report love. What will your brain report? Keep it simple and your heart and
head will thank you later.

Blend a fun little dinner at a public place, just the two of you, with
hooking-up with another couple to finish the night off. Ok, it wasn't simple
– it was compound. See how I am? Let's toast bifurcation!   (This book is
for grad students too.)

A deluge of feelings will challenge your sanity. Keep it simple

The Try Out Date
48
Strategy

"You can tell whether a man is clever by his answers. You can tell whether a man is wise by his questions."
Naguib, Mahfouz

"Men show their character in nothing more clearly than by what they find laughable."
Anon

Take a walk downtown; get some dinner, hang-out afterward at an ice cream shop where you can join another couple for a double-date and from there on to a club, a carnival, whatever. But first learn more about what he thinks is funny; learn more of what interests him about you - anything that allows the two of you to get to know each other without distractions like nosey people, loud music, drama and excitement.

Dance clubs, parties, movies all prevent easy, flowing communication where a thought is allowed to evolve and reveal the speaker's beliefs and values. You want to use your wits, feel the vibrations, and sense the intonations and nuances of his actions and reactions. Keep it simple, direct, and one on one, face to face and casual. A huge volume of information will be available for you to process if you set the stage to experience each other. You do want to get to know him, don't you? The concept, of course, is to let your good sense beat the animal magnetism to a decision on this guy. Your body wants to mate. Your soul needs a mate. You're the referee but you will begin loosing your stripes rapidly if your procreation circuit chip senses something it likes and begins shutting down your logic system and narrowing your perspective. Slippery Slope Ahead!

"Now the reason the enlightened prince and the wise general conquer the enemy whenever they move and their achievements surpass those of ordinary men is foreknowledge."
Sun Tzu, Ancient Military Commander

Looking Hot
49
Strategy

Save some trump cards for when you need them. Resist cranking up your maximum hotness for awhile; let the first couple of (try-out) dates happen *easily* without the props, the decorations and the distractions. You may soon decide that you do not want this guy "stuck on you." In fact, you may learn things in the first few try-outs that will make you wish you hadn't attracted him at all. Besides, why play your aces immediately? Wait until you learn what trump cards he has before you decide that the game is really on. Then you can show him your best game. You'll also then validate his role as pursuer and show you have recognized his pursuit.

On hearing this strategy one girl said to me, "Hey, I always dress my hottest when I'm out with a new guy. I want him to view me at my best right from the start. If the guy turns out to be a dud instead of a dude, tough luck for him." To this I would say: some duds are actually dudes, dudes who have been so taken by your awesome attractiveness that they just came unglued in your presence. You really need to step up your temperature slowly for some guys or risk watching them boil over from premature exposure, kind of like tanning. Let his melanin build up before you reveal your full sunshine or risk exploding him right out of the tanning booth.

Save some trump cards for when you need them.

Double Dates
50
Strategy

B eware the *whole* date as a double-date in the beginning. As much as they're fun they're another big distraction. Most double-dates wind up sounding like a sit-com with short sound bites and canned laughter for every silly quip, pun, exaggeration or joke anyone can think of. Double dates are a blast, don't get me wrong. They just need to be later in the evening rather than sooner …in the second phase of vetting your candidate. (Coffees are phase one.) Once you hear that his beliefs and values are okay, you'll want to observe his behavior energized – like watching him play ball on Saturday morning with the guys in his dorm or house. If that's okay too, then a double date to the amusement park, nightclub or house party should be a great time for everyone with few surprises. Drugs and alcohol, it must be said, are always a wild card potentially empowering whole new worlds of bizarre behavior. Fools rush in where angels fear to tread dept.

Not-with-standing that, celebrating your mutual discovery of each other with best friends is very cool and should easily produce maximum fun. It's just not what you do until you've shared some "face time" - been out with the guy to see how he behaves with just you to focus on. Review your purpose of the "try-out date." This is not just "Make me laugh." This is "Make me understand, believe and like you."

A combination one on one with no one else to interrupt *then* a double date to de-intensify the mood, top off the night and protect your route home safely is a shrewd strategy that can be repeated several times until its clear your sensibilities have had sufficient data to process and declare this guy is a likely bet to solo with.

Offbeat Tunes
51
Technique

It's probably a good idea to say a few words about badly out of tune instruments that translate to weird male behavior. It doesn't necessarily mean you've got a weird guy. He may just need a tune up.

Don't underrate yourself. Any female can be devastating to a male's central nervous system, and remember, your attractiveness is not solely the function of your physical self! Your sunshine has set his hormones in motion and his equilibrium may need time to adjust to your magnetic pull. So don't be alarmed; there may be a riot raging in his head. You may have delighted him to such a degree that his frivolous self, the little kid, appears. Feverish blows with your handbag won't help. You'll probably just set off another panic attack.

A calming smile is your best reaction to his strange behavior, coupled with the simple question, "Are you okay?" voiced in a serious, quiet, concerned tone. When he does something annoying again, repeat the question, this time putting your hand on his arm saying, "Are you *sure* you're okay?" He now understands his behavior is causing you *confusion*. Consistently react without emotion to every inappropriate "little kid" outbreak. Remember, his equilibrium may take some adjustment time. It's a great time to impress him with your patience. He will be impressed, and if there's any correcting it, this method will get it done the fastest.

A word of caution: Do not use a big sister tone or a motherly tone. It may call up pictures of someone he could confuse you with forever. You want to be thought of as you - special and unique. Read this thought twelve times!

"When you call upon a Thoroughbred, he gives you all the speed, strength
of heart and sinew in him.
When you call on a jackass, he kicks."
Patricia Neal

The Jerk
52
Technique

A stronger message becomes necessary when he goes into hyper-drive and you refuse to be a party to behavior that your better judgment disapproves. As his self control decreases, your self control must increase. Don't get hyper with him and blurt out commands. You don't want to trigger the warrior that reacts automatically when it senses he's under attack. He'll verbally duel with you, raising his voice to gain authority, and you'll wind up in a shouting match that will likely botch the whole date. Don't escalate the crisis; keep it manageable. Here's what I witnessed a very smart girl do one night to her fighting date. It applies well here.

Keep your style firm and non-combative. Your tone must be sincere and firm, but delivered in a *calm, slow, quiet manner.* He must be made to sense that he is dealing with a lady of unwavering character. *Do not command,* but appeal to him looking directly in his eyes so that he takes note of the way his behavior is affecting you. He needs to know what you are feeling. Talk to him sincerely using his first name. " Bob, when you _____. It makes me feel _____. This will tell him what's up with you and that it's ok to just slow down here and he won't blow the date – which may be a fear further exaggerating his drama. (Ok, so he already did. You and I know that but his demons don't.)

The key to getting his attention is to lower your voice as he raises his. He will sense that you are not competing against him and that he must listen harder to hear your words. You are causing his focus to move from broadcasting his message to understanding what you are saying. This should take some of the steam out of his behavior and prepare him for what you are about to fill in the above blanks with. More about this next.

If you have carefully adhered to the strategy of targeting public places for your first evenings out and avoided ones where alcohol and drugs will likely be present, like house parties, you should be spared this sort of encounter.

The Dishonor Maneuver
53
Opportunity

T he words you use to fill-in the blanks on how he makes you feel need to be carefully chosen for stopping power. You are not talking to a woman. Many words have much less significance to a man than you might believe, take, for instance, the two words *embarrassed* and *ashamed*. Guys rarely get embarrassed - women do that. (Ladies perspire; men sweat) Guys can relate to *shame*, though. It translates to *dishonor*. And we men want anything but dishonor!

A man's concept of dishonor comes from our warrior tradition. The warrior ethic decrees certain virtues to be inviolate. Ah... that means he gets real uncomfortable if he thinks he's causing dishonor. You can call up these images by using certain male "buzz words." Their opposites, translated to the present day are:

Past: Warrior	Present: Wimp
Gallantry	coward
Nobility	low class
Honor	shame

The trick in using them is to apply them with reference to *you*, not him. Remember, he's a warrior and an insult is a harmless attack that is automatically deflected. On the other hand, a warrior cannot tolerate a *lady's dishonor*. You only need to describe his behavior and tell him that it makes you feel shamed or low class or a coward. This is guaranteed to work on any guy worth staying with another minute. Guys can't stand a non-combative women being abused. Believe me; I've refereed more domestic arguments among couples whether unmarried or married than was necessary to learn these lessons. It isn't pretty. These observations came from real life situations where the misbehavers were sometimes drunk and sometimes sober. Life's lessons are where you find them.

Call me a student of conflict, confusion and chaos. My nightclub and restaurant were one big experiment in human behavior, and most of my ideas were pressure tested under extreme conditions. The above solution does not, however, work on spoiled, rich brats or law school students I learned. Projectile vomiting, however, does. That was probably more than you needed to know, but I saw it work. The lady got two with one shot and dispersed them both. I was impressed.

Back to the issue at hand.   Your sincerity and tone drive these words to leverage their impact; this drops his shield and sword, gets his full attention and raises serious issues in his mind. He's very likely not witnessed a lady issuing such a distress call. He may have heard his teacher or his mother use the words, but not in this context. They would be speaking as a dominant authority and, again, the reference was to him, not to her. (Two more good reasons not to assume the authority tone.) He's no doubt heard this from his father or coach though. These words are guaranteed to get his attention! They are extremely high voltage to him, especially when he's guilty, and they should be reserved for worst case scenarios only. Again it what's happening to *you*. You are feeling shame. Don't look mad – look distressed.

Once you have his attention, reassure him that you still think he has some very attractive qualities - this should allow him to turn the corner - and that you'd like to [insert another activity here] to continue enjoying his company. Notice that you haven't told him to *stop*; you've just let him know that you are degraded by the scene and are supplying a positive alternative. "I'd love to go for a coffee or to the Union for a bite." Otherwise call a cab. You can always retreat to the ladies room to make the call. Let management know you'd like an escort to it.

Any future discussion of a date should cause you to recap your feelings of the last one. The presumption is that he will alter his behavior to accommodate you. He gets to test your patience, but your policy is "enough is enough." If the use of alcohol or drugs is the problem, suggest your solution. If you are not accommodated on the next date – which I wouldn't recommend - tell him that the person you had agreed to be with is not the person he is delivering, and that you are not interested in that person or perhaps in either person if one can't control the other. It's the Dr. Jekyll and Mr. Hyde syndrome, and you are not obligated to put up with it. You do have the local taxicab number on your cell, right?

Physical Distractions
54
Strategy

As you lie in bed at night, your hands behind your head, staring up at the stars printed on the bottom sheet hanging over the edge of your roommate's loft, you begin to focus on this new guy. You picture him in your mind's eye. You want to do some evaluating but find yourself thinking about the way he wrinkles his nose when he gets nervous. His physical self starts to work on you. By the third date you realize this guy's got you. You started out looking for a certain kind of guy, one that looks a certain way - a certain height, a certain hair, hands, and eyes. But you wind up being completely distracted by a different guy whose spirit lights up his whole being and sets your heart on fire. That's a great start. But suppose that's as good as it gets. Suppose there's a big zero hiding behind that magic facade? Suppose he winds up breaking your heart? Hey, it wouldn't be the first time a gal got fooled. What then?

> "I hold it true, what'er befall;
> I feel it, when I sorrow most;
> 'Tis better to have loved and lost
> Than never to have loved at all."
> Alfred Lord Tennyson

How do you guard against falling in love with Mr. Almost? You have only one defense - *Recognize the bad traits before the blue eyes work their magic on you.* No matter how perceptive you've trained yourself to be, cupid may tag you before reality and all of the facts become clear. Love at first sight is cause for more than celebration – it's cause for alarm. How do you protect your heart? The truth is that you *can't* always protect it.

> "We choose our joys and sorrows long before we experience them."
> Kahlil Gibran

This Ain't the Next Rose Ceremony

You may have observed on The Bachelor/ette – the TV reality (or at least semi-reality) series where time constraints require one to rapidly summon one's feelings for the other person and announce them sooner than later. In television-land you have only a few, short dates – with cameras rolling – to amp-up your feelings or risk being perceived as emotionally distant by the one who would measure your sincerity and passion.

Hopefully the context of your romances won't be hyper-accelerated with cameras recording every breath as you rush your feelings to a hasty conclusion, summon your best courage, and blurt out a proper sound byte on how you are falling in love… all to avoid the risk of losing at the next rose ceremony. Whew, better stick to the real world!

"To fall in love is easy, even to remain in it is not difficult; our human loneliness is cause enough.
But it is a hard quest worth making to find a comrade through whose steady presence one becomes steadily the person one desires to be."
Anna Louise Strang

Charisma
55
Opportunity

S ome people have such amazing charisma that their powers of attraction cannot be anticipated. The effects are sometimes immediate, and often prolonged. However, we can vaccinate you and accelerate your recovery... that is, once you regain consciousness! When you finally wake up and begin thinking rationally again, you will rapidly add things up. Remember? You've trained yourself to recognize what really matters.

Your ability to recognize positive traits will give you a perspective on what this guy is really worth to you. Add some courage and say your goodbyes. "Time's a wasting!" Somebody NEW AND SPECIAL is waiting to discover you and YOU may be keeping him waiting! Hoping to fall in love is good, but not, however, when applied to the wrong person. One must be willing to withdraw the wish and continue the hunt elsewhere.

In short, being in love doesn't make it right.

"A very small degree of hope is sufficient to cause the birth of love."
Stendhal

Recycle 'Em
56
Strategy

"When I see a bird that walks like a duck and swims like a duck and quacks like a duck, I call that bird a duck."
James Whitcomb Riley

There are really only three stages to sorting-out guys: interviews, try-out dates and the relationship. So what to do when you realize that your love isn't right? You move on. You've seen it before… a girl or guy you know finally wakes up one day and dumps their other half. Their incompatibility was obvious to everyone, and you figure this strange bird is destined to walk the face of the earth lonely forever. But lo and behold, you spot him or her later with someone new, happy as can be. You observe them closely and realize they appear to be a perfect match. "Oh my gosh – who 'da thunk?"

It's likely alien spacecraft have crashed on earth over the millennium and therefore possible that their descendants…. okay, but you get the idea. Just goes to show that "one woman's bum is another woman's beau." Some people are just meant to be together. So hurry up and lose this slightly or terribly wrong guy. When? As soon as you realize you are not meant to be together. Remember, the quicker you sort 'em out, the sooner you meet Mr. Right. Don't worry… Your reject is someone else's Rembrandt.

Think galactically – recycle!

"Success is how high you bounce when you hit bottom."
General George Patton

"He conquers who endures." –Persius

Exit Science
57
Technique

"Illegitimis non carborundum."
"Don't let the bastards grind you down."
Gen. Joseph Stilwell

S o you're at the "just dating" or try-out date stage. Life's a breeze. In
fact, you may be going out with several guys. Just have fun and pay
particular attention to their character traits and talents. Are they compatible
with you? If you want to get really scientific about this thing, which is a
good idea when you start to feel confused, just get out the old legal pad and
list their traits - all of them, one every other line. (see appendices in back for
lists and ideas)

Rate each item on a scale of one to five. Put the score in the margin. Put the
pad in the drawer and look at it again after you've had a good night's sleep.
Are the ratings still fair? Okay, so how good does he look on paper? Chances
are the emotional side of you has been failing to admit some of the things
the logical side has been trying to bring to your attention. Or worse, the
logical side of you has been in such control that it's not allowing you to feel
anything for this guy. This is always a learning experience, and sometimes it
greatly accelerates decisions. Try it. It's good to be in touch with your
perceptions and your feelings.

"Character cannot be developed in ease and quiet. Only through experience
of trial and suffering can the soul be strengthened,
ambition inspired, and success achieved."
Helen Keller

Predictability
58
Technique

I can feel you getting impatient... How can you tell how this guy will measure up in the weeks and months to come? Unfortunately the future contains unforeseen circumstances. You cannot accurately forecast human behavior, even if you knew what the future holds. You can only prepare yourself with an accurate picture of his traits and talents as they exist now and begin nurturing them as you observe his responsiveness. If he responds to your sunshine and grows in your light. then you have a good beginning. If he returns your nurturing with his own, then you have a great beginning. Only by being a keen observer of today's, tomorrow's, next month's, and next year's behavior may you begin to be assured of what the future holds for you. That's the best anyone can ask for in a prediction.

As for increasing the accuracy of your interpretations, there are several things that you can do to help it along. You look all around him and see what he sees. You compare his vision with yours. Are *his* eyes in focus? You meet his friends and observe their traits and talents. You compare what he sees in them with what you see in them. Conversely, you attempt to see what they see in your guy. Is everyone seeing the same picture? You meet his parents and begin recognizing his traits in them. Now you know you're seeing him correctly. If you see his dominant traits in his parents, then you know he did not recently acquire them and your sight is near 20/20.

He is what he appears to be. If, however, you clearly sense traits in his parents that you feared were present in him, then you likely have a fault in the construction of your violin.

Can you repair it? You alone are the final judge. Years from now you may face the mirror and call yourself as a witness to testify regarding your decision, so make it a good one.

"No change of circumstances can repair a defect of character."
Ralph Waldo Emerson

Pleading Temporary Infatuation
59
Opportunity

As in any mirror trial, you - the jury - will decide whether a reasonable person would have made the same decision. Make sure he's got dreamy blue eyes if he's a cheat, a liar or a coward. You will need to plead "temporary infatuation"... a small consolation if divorce and kids become part of the package. If you suspect you may be in denial, call Dr Laura. Being disciplined publicly on the radio is perhaps what it's going to take.

Are you beginning to see how things can go either way? You need to enjoy dating with the certain knowledge that at some point in time you alone will have to decide if this guy's Mr. Right. Get honest with yourself as quickly as you can. You deserve every break you can get, so develop a charitable side and listen carefully to your hunches. Someone who knows you very well, YOU, has something important to say. Listen to what she is thinking. There's your answer.

"Never try to teach a pig to sing; it's a waste of time and it annoys the pig".
Robert A. Heinlein

"Well, I can wear heels now."
Nicole Kidman
(After Tom Cruise divorce)

Character & Virtue
60
Technique

"Besides pride, loyalty, discipline, heart, and mind, confidence is the key to all the locks." Joe Paterno, Penn State

A person's positive character traits I'll refer to as their "virtue set" - a set of virtues calculated to serve the beliefs and values of a person. Here's a list to check him against. Any one that turns up missing is likely to immediately disqualify the guy. If you must have a tattoo, put these on the inside of your eyelids so that when you blink in disbelief at what's coming out of his mouth you'll have a handy reference.

Courage Integrity Humor Sensitivity Curiosity Dependability Self Esteem   Good Will   Intelligence   Morality   Compassion   Energy Patience Empathy Positive Attitude Egotism Resilience Fair Play Possibility-Thinking Optimism Determination Humility Courtesy

There are lots more – take a peak at appendices in back for lists and ideas. These qualities enable him, they are features of his character. Here is his "self." Here is the person, cleverly disguised as man. Here, therefore, is the target. Below the surface of every guy lie the traits that you will attempt to discover. Who is he, really? You can begin answering this question as soon as you can begin to focus on his core values and not just the good looks, cute smile and the dreamy eyes that captivate you.

By the stories he tells you must assess the integrity of his virtues. Do they stand up to difficulty? Is there courage in his convictions, or does his behavior convict his stories of courage?

"Courage is not simply one of the virtues, but the form of every virtue at the testing point." Clive Staples Lewis

Assembling His Composite
61
Technique

T he first order of business in any relationship is for both parties to begin to understand each other. You trade experiences and share laughs; tell stories and get a sense for what the other's life is like. What does he see in you from what you have made available for his examination? Your hair, your smile, your laugh, your intelligence, your looks, your ideals, your dreams, and *your behavior toward him* evoke a composite impression in his mind When it happens to involve the romantically inclined who appear compatible for courtship, then you can't wait to discover the answer. Both of you will be working overtime assembling these puzzle parts to create an accurate picture of the other person's character and personality.

Morsel Mining

If your appraisal of his character and personality fit your criteria, make you feel warm and fuzzy, satisfy both your head and your heart, then proceed to validate the role you see him providing in a relationship with you.

You: "I can see the two of us in a relationship down the road." (Admittedly, it could be a short road, but factor some extra time in there for the revelations that are sure to follow his initial sales pitch to you.)

Him: "A relationship, eh? What sort would that be?"

You: "The romantic kind."

Him: "Whew, I was hoping that would be the one – but a guy never knows with ladies these days."

You: "Oh, have you had some ladies use you for other things?"

Him: "Ah, yes! Like furniture mover, bicycle mechanic, jealousy pawn, chemistry tutor, counselor… In your case, I prefer the role of boyfriend."

You: "Boyfriend, eh? Seems like you might fit the part. What a coincidence; I'll be holding auditions this month! Let's start with *friend* and see how that goes."

Him: "All month?"

You: "How long are *your* auditions?"

Him: "Oh, well it depends."

You: (you raise an eyebrow) "I see, and what criteria do you use?"

Each morsel is a clue. The first "audition criteria" he states is *smile*. You repeat his statements.

You: "Smile. I see. And what does smile do for you?"

You and he can have all kinds of fun as you bore into his mind, examining some of his statements and having sport with others that seem humorous to him. You take turns, like tennis, serving sometimes, other times returning the ball. You're learning more than one might suspect. You are learning how you both take turns, how you play together, if he likes to hear your opinion or just his own.

But remember to do a lot more listening than talking. You already live with you. You want to learn if you'd like to live with him. What are his passions? Make him fully energize his reasoning circuits and chase around his brain for answers. Is he nimble, alert, quick and sensible... or confused, irrational and slow? Does his brain enamor you or put you off? Is he cute or a slug?

"A girl's gotta do what a girl's gotta do." Anonymous

"All is fair in love and war" Lyric, Al Dubin

Critique Him
62
Technique

"Sexiness wears thin after a while and beauty fades, but to be married to a man who makes you laugh every day, ah, now that's a real treat."
Joanne Woodward

Only by putting him through his paces will he really perform for you. And will he do it willingly or begrudgingly? Is he enthusiastic to have you as his rider, prancing with spirit and reacting to your every command, or is he willfully resisting your direction to answer his questions? Does he have something to hide or nothing to offer? Keep pushing his buttons. If he is enamored with you, he will enjoy it. Keep it 90% his responses and 10% your asking. Resist his efforts to turn the tables on you. While it's fair to trade info more evenly at the initial coffee shop interviews, the first try-out dates need to rapidly inform you about him. After all, you need to disqualify him if necessary - sooner rather than later – before Cupid gets to you.

The idea is to let your brain signal that his physicality – blue eyes, broad shoulders, square jaw, cute dimples, wavy hair – are no bargain in light of the unattractive, put-you-down morsels falling from his lips. You want to become intimate with his thinking before your heart races out of control and spins you into another go-nowhere romance with another no-match-for-you guy. Do you agree? Once your endorphins release, your logic systems become semi-paralyzed and cease to serve you. Nature is compelling you to mate as soon as it, not you, perceives a match; so you're in an information gathering race, and talking about yourself is counter productive at this, the try-out stage.

"Listen or thy tongue will keep thee deaf." Native American Proverb

"When you choose your friends, don't be short-changed by choosing personality over character." W. Somerset Maugham

Subtle Echo
63
Technique

Looking for differences is probably more important at first than looking for similarities. Core value differences can undermine a couple's relationship faster than similarities can bind it together. So be alert for statements or behavior, perhaps only subtle, that echo in your head. They can also reveal larger issues down the road.

For an interesting perspective, consider this trait difference within a larger context. So your new guy tells a little white lie here and there. You wouldn't do it, but it's really no big deal, right? Imagine this man as the father of your children. Now imagine him reflecting that same degree of honesty at the supper table in front of your family on Thanksgiving, or at your child's school in the principle's office. How does that difference feel now, in these real world scenarios?

"Always design a thing by considering it in its next larger context - a chair in a room, a room in a house, a house in an environment, an environment in a city plan." Eliel Saarinen

By focusing on his beliefs and values, his character traits, and his virtues, you begin spotting them in use and know they exist. The ones you like should produce your best, most positive reactions. That way you *maintain his focus* on the features that drive your feelings for him. He knows what you admire in him, so he exercises those character traits more. Like the violin that is especially melodious in certain ranges, you frequently compliment the musician for selecting the songs (behaviors) that feature those ranges.

He is reminded of what he excels at and what you enjoy in him. Even before you get to the stage of putting your arms around him, you send him the message. He can now settle down and begin playing the correct role. Your frequent messages reinforce his positive behavior.

"Love can sometimes be magic. But magic can sometimes...
just be an illusion." Javan

Sometimes people fall in love with people they shouldn't marry.
Anonymous

Section VI

Sorting Things Out

"Choosing the Right Instrument"

Role Recognition
Role Validation
He Made the Cut
Dream Discovery
Dream Recognition
Commitment
Your Dream
Commitment Reaction
When to Celebrate
Recognizing False Harmony
Natural Chemistry
Animal Magnetism
Coincidence

HARMONY

LOVE is the child of harmony.
Harmony comes with accommodation.
Accommodation begins with recognition.
Recognition confers admiration & respect.
Admiration & respect build self confidence.
Self confidence is the engine of accomplishment.
Accomplishment is self actualizing.
Self actualization is fulfillment.
Fulfillment is harmony.
Harmony is bliss.

Role Recognition
64
Technique

"**D**o you like me?" "What do you like about me?" "Are we a match?" These are the first questions on everybody's mind. Everyone wants respect (recognition), and you are both just dying to know what the other one sees in them. He wants to know if you really see him as a potential mate, or perhaps only a brother, a father, or a helper - someone to help you in the chem. lab, someone to fix your car or bicycle, someone who knows a guy that she'd like to go out with. His first goal then is to be *validated* as a potential mate, and certainly your curiosity seeks these answers as well. Both of you are looking for your *role* to be validated so that you may proceed in the appropriate fashion. Just what are his intentions?

Probing discussions will attempt to reveal the roles that the other person expects to find in a mate as well as what roles they think they can provide. Is there a *comfortable* place for you to fulfill yourself? Does this place suggest a picture that compares favorably with the one that you'd pictured before you met him? If not, can his idea be changed? "Is he... an accommodator?" He may or may not be, according to how you interpret his initial behavior. Remember, the signals you get could be entirely false if your magnetic pull has seriously affected his equilibrium. He may be spending sleepless nights thinking about you, wondering why he is behaving so unlike himself. Better to reserve judgment. Give him a chance to settle down. We'll deal with his ability to accommodate soon enough. First let's see if you like him.

"The will to win is important, but the will to prepare is vital."
Joe Paterno, Head Coach, Penn State

Role Validation
65
Technique

"The sweetest of all sounds is praise." Xenophon

N ow let's presume you've gone out with this guy a few times, that you've spotted a lot of positive traits, and that he's passed your entrance requirements. Now you're ready for a little archery. Good thing you've been practicing on unsuspecting pedestrians these last many months, huh? It's time for an arrow aimed at his provider-protector role.

The object is to let him know that you see him as a potential mate. You want to validate your intentions with him. This small show of recognition should get you some serious admiration and respect and give him the confidence to relax and reveal more of himself.

Let me show you how simple playing the first romantic note on his violin might be. It's as simple as telling him how much you appreciate having him open a door, pull out your chair, compliment you on your hair... whatever he's done these last several dates that has you impressed. What little thing has he done that "touched" you?

Okay, here's what it might sound like in a real life situation - You've just been seated, and the waiter is expected to appear at your table any minute. You look up from the menu and wait for his eyes to meet yours. You smile and say, in a slightly quieter than normal tone...

You: "You know, Billy-Joe-Bob (always use his name), when you chased my parasol across the football field just as the other team kicked that field goal, or shared that toothpick with me at the county fair (whatever is gentlemanly where you come from), you sure made me feel like a lady!"

Now give him a wink to seal it, and you've punched his ticket. You then change subjects before this little drama catches his hair on fire.

You: "Hey, what looks good on the menu, Billy? Have you tried the tangerine bean dip here?"

Him: "Dad-gum it, Cheryl Lee-Ann, you are one sweet sugar plum darlin'!"

(Sometimes I get carried away with the dialogue, sorry.)

What an amazing bow! It plays notes on a violin and shoots arrows, too! Okay, recall how potent a recognition arrow can be. It's a simple message but powered by DNA (harmony is in our genes). Make sure your eyes are meeting. Yes, this simple statement will definitely get his attention, but when he collects himself he'll know you recognize his accommodating behavior.

Your manner and tone will communicate admiration & respect for his role behavior as the love prospect and not some other role. It will charge him up at first but will ultimately relax him, allowing him to feel more secure so that he'll begin to act more naturally.

It will also tune-up his manners! Sound like progress you can live with? What you're not seeing is the positive force field that's not only attracting good things to the relationship but also displacing the opportunity for negativity to materialize. I know that sounds a little zany, but good stuff attracts good stuff; and the good stuff literally pushes the bad stuff right out of your zone.

The longer you are on the planet, the more obvious this opportunity will become. The more you actively promote goodwill, the more it visits you. It's real easy to get used to it. Remember to say thank you to all the angels in that great control tower in the sky when you close your eyes at night. Everyone loves recognition.

He Made the Cut
66
Strategy

T he fact that you validated his role tells me he's on the team. He made the cut! He's been accepted as the one to pursue and be pursued by. You now can be mildly confident of starting a relationship with a much higher potential for success than had you not done your homework on this guy – and he on you. Why go out to have fun with someone you won't like and after one date feel awful for the experience?

Seems like simple reasoning, but people buy clothes all the time, pack them in their suitcase and show up for a wedding in another city on the morning of the event only to discover they can't button the thing. This guy can button. Now let's see how he wears.

You've been acting as a screening agent looking to book a prospect, and now you can relax that persona and be more like yourself. You'll continue to ask questions and evaluate behavior, but now they will blend into sports, movies, parties, double-dates, road trips, walks and talks. In the midst of it all, you should be actively discovering each other's life goals and attempting to coach each other's progress along those paths. Ah, the magic of helping enable dreams!

"And the day came when the risk to remain tight in a bud was more painful than the risk it took to blossom." Anais Nin

Dream Discovery
67
Technique

Y ou both have passionate feelings for certain pursuits. Sometimes these passions are suppressed by circumstances, past or present. They are not always on the surface or even known to their owners. Dream stealers, nay-sayers, ankle-biters, and pessimists take their toll on our dreams, and sometimes they wreak such destruction that those dreams end up gathering cobwebs in a shoebox in a forgotten corner of our mind. It's understandable then, that it sometimes takes more than a little detective work to uncover someone's forgotten passions, resuscitate them and then piece together the dreams that could accompany them.

By hearing moments of joy proclaimed through another's stories, we sometimes visit the roots of those underlying passions. Imagine the value of helping to uncover lost dreams and then offering to help accommodate their rebirth as a primary life goal – perhaps even a career? The confidence building that will occur when you recognize the character traits and unique talents that a person possesses will motivate you to first cheerlead, then coach those potentials into reality. That's the inspiration another needs to do the same for you, with a little coaching and cheerleading. Why not choose a truly empowering and passionate relationship over one with just passion?

Play 'Find Your Passion'

Those walks, talks and relaxing moments at the coffee shop can be the play yard of dreams. "So what are you so passionate about, Todd, that if you won the 10 million dollar lottery tomorrow - and *after* you had bought all the cool cars and clothes, visited all the great vacation spots and built your dream castle, had a year to party and play – after all that, what would you just love to do more than anything else you can think of that would be productive?

What would you do with the canvas known as "the rest of your life?" He may be dumbfounded; then again he may not be. Whether he speaks now or needs a day or two to think it over is something you can accommodate.

This topic of conversation is a great mechanism for coaxing out dreams. "Possibility thinking" is a first step to talk about what fabulous dreams the two of you have and hear their similarities and differences. It gives you a beginning point for talking about your future with a person that, until now, you probably don't have any history with. So actually, the future is what you share.

Talking about it jumps the conversation over the present (which is only moments long) to a place where you might possibly want to share the rest of your lives together. In short, it's stimulating and informative to talk about high school and childhood... but conversation about what *might* be can *truly be* empowering!

Okay, your turn. This is your chance to show him who you really are, where you're going and what all the scenery along the way might look like. Don't have a dream with details yet? Imagine one. Make it up. Because it's a dream it can be as uniquel as you are. So break out of now and imagine you in the future.

What would you really like to do – in your wildest dreams - that would use your talents, challenge your imagination, stretch your courage and guarantee a place in your college's Who's Who List twenty years from now? Share it with him.

It sometimes takes more than a little detective work to uncover someone's forgotten passions, resuscitate them and then piece together the dreams that could accompany them.

Dream Recognition
68
Technique

"So many of our dreams at first seem impossible, then they seem
improbable, and then, when we summon the will,
they soon become inevitable."
Christopher Reeve

How Do I Create My Dream?

Maybe it's to own your own company that consults, counsels,
negotiates, finances, creates, designs, educates, or motivates, other
companies or organizations. Maybe you work for somebody - a famous
person, as their assistant. Maybe you work for a Fortune 500 company as
CEO, CFO, chief counsel, landscape architect, chemist, auditor, human
resources or product planner. Maybe you travel the world with a microscope
or sit as chief programmer for the next Hubble Telescope. Will you travel a
lot or work out of your home? Will you have a small or large staff, and how
many direct assistants will you need? Are you a people person or do you like
your privacy? This is more than a casual conversation about what you might
like to do tomorrow. You really need to think about "what if" and....

Dream Key

Here's the key to unlocking the secret – What would you happily, joyfully,
gladly do... even if the pay was minimal? What would make you so
intoxicatingly happy you'd do it darn near free? That's the key. That's your
dream. Now fill in the details by closing your eyes and seeing yourself in the
course of your day, in moments of achievement and passion. What are you
wearing? Who are you talking to? Where are you located? What does your
work space look like? This is what you tell this poor, unprepared guy who is
about to get a mega-volt of amazing, unbelievable you! Whatever really
makes you come alive is the part of life you picture yourself chasing after,
and from your vantage point right now, this is what your dream looks like.
Everyday brings new information that tweaks the dream morphing it once
again. It just continues to fit you a little better with every new revelation.
You never stop growing and neither does your dream.

Your dream should be good enough to base a movie on it. This is time travel in High Definition, titled: "Thrill to My Dreams." It's an action-packed adventure demonstrating - get ready for this, your talents and character traits challenged in your most imaginative model of the *supreme* career. He needs to picture you advancing the progress of your favorite art or science for charity or profit while you share the thrills of the challenge and adventure. You might depersonalize it by speaking in the third person. Drama is good. You make him sense your anticipation and how it makes "her" mind come alive as you chronicle what "she" thinks. Your task here is to begin the process of recognizing that each day will dawn on the freshest version of your grandest vision of your highest and best use. You finish with …"And that person is me!"

"The future belongs to those who believe in the beauty of their dreams."
Eleanor Roosevelt

Commitment
69
Strategy

Okay, let's do a "what if?" and say that your relationship with this guy has passed the initial pre-date interviews. You've spent some quality time talking with him in addition to 5 - 10 of dates. His character reflects your ideals, his personality syncs nicely with yours, and you're starting to get the hots for him. You're at the stage where you want to get mentally intimate by sharing your dreams, and you sense in him a depth and maturity that screams soul-mate. Let's add to that... and here's where we may loose some of you but that's ok because "shock and awe" is not for everyone, yet potential commitment could be an issue. Here's a little scenario that can be an early predictor of your future with this guy. Admittedly, it takes a lot of nerve to do...but hey, I'll let you be the judge. Here goes... You first share your amazing dream for your life with him, and then you wait about twenty minutes then boldly advance the question:

"Is this the kind of dream you could support in a mate –not necessarily me – but in someone, Bill?

When he hears this challenge, he may get religion... yours! He may well say yes. Positive minded, "going places" people love to participate in grand adventures, especially when they can share the stage. If he does, you are beginning your relationship with him from a very special place - the future - and it is here and now. No matter what he says, he knows he may well have met his match, figuratively and otherwise. You are not to be underestimated.

In any event, his reaction will be revealing... very. So you must study him closely for the next few minutes. He may tip his hand. For instance, is he calm or nervous, conversant or quiet, animated or frozen? Does he hesitate, palpitate and stammer, speak in phrases, sentences or paragraphs because of your question? Guys are allowed to be nervous, especially if they suddenly find themselves perched on the edge of a potentially life changing precipice. The uptake in adrenalin alone can be staggering, especially coupled in the presence of wonderful, amazing you.

Your Dream
70
Technique

Y ou've cleverly captured his imagination as your sunshine beams onto the widescreen of his mind. He will bend to this sunshine instinctively. You've just played a concerto for him on your own violin. If your passion is music to his ears, you'll see it in his eyes and posture. In any case, he'll now see your dream, be inspired by your vision, and your image will be clarified.

Obviously, it would be wise to give this dream some mental deliberation – some possibility thinking, some creative preparation - before dimming the house lights, packing his face with popcorn and letting your video clip rip. It doesn't matter that you don't actually know yet what you will do. It only matters that you are prepared to fill the void with something intelligently passionate that you would love to do. Don't be practical - that's too limiting.

Remember, your potential is limitless! Imagine yourself with miraculous resources. There is a very good chance you will astound and inspire yourself! What dream would you attempt if you knew you could not fail? Your unconscious mind would love a plan with some starting details to begin its work as your master navigator and hunch communicator.

So, how did it go? Your communication was full of enthusiasm and substance. You artfully brushed a vision on the canvas of his mind; you didn't bore him with trivial patter. You have accommodated his curiosity; he recognizes your passion and need to exercise it. You've given him something to chew on. Let it rest for now. He'll need some time for this one.

You now have something special in common, something exciting to talk about – your grandest possibilities! It'll be important to discuss any changes in your goals as quickly as they occur. Exercising flexibility in your plans indicates your ability to change as some doors close and others open. You must become an opportunity thinker. Don't be afraid to wonder out loud and let him be a part of your planning. Remember, you are working on becoming a team.

Actively request his assistance in coaching you and ask his permission to coach him as well as you prepare to share your changing visions and advance along your dream paths. Remember, every great journey begins with a first step. If yours doesn't, break it down into one. You will be given some incredible tools in the coming last chapters. Get ready for the ride of your life!

"Chance favors the prepared mind."
Louis Pasteur

"Go confidently in the direction of your dreams.
Live the life you have imagined."
Henry David Thoreau

Commitment Reaction
71
Strategy

D o not display your dream and then immediately follow up with your "commitment" question. If you do, you won't be able to separate his reaction to your dream from his reaction to your commitment question. Specific goals are controlling these experiments, and the first is to listen and watch him react to each: one stimulus, one response. Let twenty minutes go by to allow his feelings and ideas react to your dream. As well, give yourself a fair appraisal time for his dream.

Let him talk himself out on it, and then tell him what it was that you thought he said and how it made you feel. Revelations of your grandest dreams should be provided in a proper, controlled setting, as an opportunity to communicate clearly and be heard and watched.

If he reacts to your questions about your dream (not the commitment) with something you didn't want to hear, don't despair. There's always the possibility it was not his true reaction but a reflex action. You may have blown his mind with the quality and or quantity of your dream and caught him totally unprepared. So don't get uptight right away. On the other hand, if he is just a dream crusher and actively mocks your grand design with ridicule or disbelief, head for the fire escape!

That being said... don't underestimate the lengths a person will go to expand their horizon and reach their potential. The atmosphere of harmony that surrounds you may well rub off on him. Once he feels the power of that recognition and feels his dreams coming into focus, he may well become your enthusiastic supporter.

He may come to recognize that accommodating your dreams could very easily become part of a workable system for attaining his dreams, too!

And by commitment I refer to a relationship with you. Not the big M. Are we horsing around here or would you like to ride along with me and see where this goes?

When to Celebrate
72
Strategy

What results do you achieve when you observe a talent exhibited, a character strength displayed, an instinct confirmed, an obstacle overcome or a goal attained, and you cheer and explain why you admire them for it? You get two results - recognition for yourself and courage for your partner. Since you are aware of these magical powers and he is probably not, you are free to demonstrate them initially for his encouragement and later for his education. You'd like the procedure returned, right? Since you have been polishing your recognition skills about campus these many long days, you will no doubt slay him with your ability to come to regular summary judgments on the tasty little performances he displays as your relationship continues.

For maximum effect, you should hold back, a smidge, your reactions to his staged dramas so that you can totally come unglued for his impromptu stunts – the ones that really reveal his character strengths. The former celebrates his imagination, the latter his goodness. So now where are you? Well, you're making good progress. You've qualified this guy, theoretically anyway. Now it's time to get to know him a little better. This time let nature take its course. It's the mystical way the subconscious mind sorts things out by mixing the delicious details of your relationship with the subtle sensitivities of your personalities.

Once your feelings surface, you can apply all this strategy to see if things still make sense. The only thing you have to do to let it work is just add time. Since we're still in the qualifying stages with this guy, let's investigate some of the possibilities you're likely to encounter. The more realistic and objective you can be about your budding relationship, the better it will be for the both of you.

Recognizing False Harmony
73
Opportunity

F alse harmony is like junk food (simple carbs) for the heart. It's a delight to the tongue and forestalls the need for real food, but when the last of it leaves your bloodstream there's an abrupt crash. Its effect can be a shock. A lot of people chow-down on false harmony because they think it feels satisfying, therefore it must be lasting. It's been around forever and is great for making babies, but when it crashes there's sometimes more than one mouth to feed.

People speak sometimes of "natural chemistry" and "animal magnetism" binding two people together. The first, natural chemistry, describes a relationship that exhibits harmony effortlessly. Two people get along famously without even trying. Your energy levels, dispositions, beliefs and feelings, especially integrity are remarkably similar - outstanding beginning. The chemistry does the meshing for you. The second, animal magnetism, describes the compulsive pull of physical attraction that draws one to another. A third situation can be called serendipity, meaning karma, kismet, destiny, or fate leading two lives to intersect and "fall into" a relationship. We'll refer to it unromantically as coincidence to help maintain a minor semblance of objectivity here.

What these three conditions, separate or in tandem, share is the uncanny ability to create a strong but sometimes false sense of lasting love. The rest of the time they create magic. Let's deal with the bad news first. The logic that reasons that "where there is smoke, there is fire" is the same logic that suggests there is love where any of these three situations present themselves. While it's not unusual to find any or all of the three present at the altar, any or all don't guarantee a "match." A divorce down the road should not be ruled out if these are all that the relationship has going for it. Let's take a closer look.

Natural Chemistry
74
Opportunity

In the first case, "natural chemistry," you feel like two peas in a pod. You seem to think the same and act the same. This is unusual, and yet similar backgrounds, beliefs and values can produce the effect. Okay, okay - in your case it's more than that. You come from entirely different backgrounds and all of your friends say it's uncanny how cool the two of you are together. Don't jump off the deep end. You've read this far, read the rest. Continue discovering his string set and teach him to discover yours.

Besides romantic walks are there caring talks - the ones that deal with who each of you are now and how each can help enable the other's dreams? Does this feeling of harmony that exists function on accommodation, the kind that assists your mental growth? If the answer is yes, then it sounds like you've got the elements of the harmony chain reaction. You know how the reaction is supposed to work... Does it? (Recognition of goals suggesting accommodation triggering admiration and respect causing courage to enable one's potential to evolve and become fulfilled.) If you're simply always on the same wavelength, giggling at the same times, beware... a shallow connection will not last long.

"Sometimes people fall in love with people they shouldn't marry."
Anonymous

(Bears repeating, spread the word.)

Animal Magnetism
75
Opportunity

In the second instance of attraction, the smoke is coming from your burning desire: "animal magnetism." Your body wants to reproduce and apparently acquired a target donor. End of story. The romance you feel are the hormones pumping euphoria into your bloodstream to act as the catalyst – you now feel overwhelming convinced that this is good. You are "swept off your feet" and compelled to procreate. You have become a pawn in nature's plan. Your logic system is awash in emotion. No help there.

Perhaps you can picture your babies with his dimples. But suppose his dimples are recessive every other generation and your twins will share his father's overbite instead. However, recognizing the dynamics of your and his marvelous gene pool, I will concede that science may supercede love in your case. Be sure to check the donor box on your driver licenses.

On the other hand, if there's no more to it than just making a beautiful couple and beautiful babies, better think again. Is he the kind of guy that after hearing your dream has become enthused to coach you, cheer you, and be your biggest fan? Or does he just want to mate and grab a beer with the guys? Somebody better be projecting the human consequences of behaving like animals.

"Sexiness wears thin after a while and beauty fades, but to be married to a man who makes you laugh every day, ah, now that's a real treat."
Joanne Woodward

Coincidence
76
Opportunity

Ah "coincidence," what a splendid proof for all things ordained in heaven. You meet in a college town and it turns out that not only are your parent's cottages on the same lake, but your moms were in the same sorority. It's fate. How about this one that happened to me... I walked out of a bar one night (before I was married) accompanying a girl to her car I had been dancing with at a club. As we stepped outside and discovered the most beautiful sky of the summer, she pointed up into the heavens and said, "Let's find our shooting star." Immediately it appeared, *exactly* where she was pointing. She was really nice and I thought, "Man, there's got to be something happening here!" Nope. It lasted three dates.

I have to admit, I'm a romantic dreamer who wants to trust in such signs. I believe the supernatural forces that watch over me can't wait to slip me hints. What I've come to realize, however, is that certain suburbs of the supernatural world are filled with pixies, goblins, and fairies that don't have the comedy channel on their cable yet. What they do have is a finely tuned sense of humor that favors us with the occurrence of these "coincidences" for no other reason than to titillate their twisted little funny bones. Nothing so excites them as a cleverly laid plot to encourage our hormones to play tricks on us. You've been punk'd!

These clever little mischief makers are at the height of their humor when playing the evil cupid. You must be forever on guard concerning romance as the mightiest of their mischief materializes when they plot to attract the mismatched to commit marriage. Be wariest in the springtime when they migrate to the meadows near campus and become intoxicated with the evening dew. The villainy they hatch under these dampish conditions is well documented and a testament to their clever instincts. Their breath can charm the strangest behavior, so take care to cover your nose when inhaling the night air as the stars seem to twinkle just for the two of you.

You must be forever on guard concerning romance as the mightiest of their mischief materializes when they plot to attract the mismatched to commit marriage.

Section VII

Courtship
Playing Duets

Happy
Enabling Rightful Evolution
Confidante
Recognizing You
Accentuate the Positive
Accentuate the Positive
Flattery Encouraged
Feather Your Nest
Robust Self Worth
Guts
Naked like a Sandbar

"It would be so cool to create a harness, dude, designed just for you and when you were in it every cool part of you would just be maxed-out and people would be in awe of what you could really do."
Iggy & Imagineers

HARMONY

LOVE is the child of harmony.
Harmony comes with accommodation.
Accommodation begins with recognition.
Recognition confers admiration & respect.
Admiration & respect build self confidence.
Self confidence is the engine of accomplishment.
Accomplishment is self actualizing.
Self actualization is fulfillment.
Fulfillment is harmony.
Harmony is bliss.

Happy

77

Opportunity

When making everyday important decisions in the midst of a changing world, one must always consider the players. Their strings determine what songs they can and should play. If the decision calls for songs (a career), and one person can't play or even enjoy hearing the other person play, then you don't have a duet. If you don't have a duet, you don't have a couple in harmony.

You must be able to relate to and project what the other's dream may mean to your lifestyle. Might he be constantly traveling or working the night shift for the first years? Do these worst case scenarios fit with your plans?

This may seem like an oversimplification, but the fact remains that each person has to be happy. When we are happy certain vital inner cords are resonating harmonically. The more often the focus of your thinking and activities touches your core, the more often a happy song will be heard playing in your hearts. If you both are happy then only the future remains to be experienced. Bliss can only be now, and that means playing songs that are not just compatible with your personality but actually engage it.

You must create this maxed-out vision of yourself with your imagination if you are to see what an amazing life you could experience. What a concept.

"It would be so cool to create a harness, dude, designed just for you and when you were in it every cool part of you would just be maxed-out and people would be in awe of what you could really do."
Iggy & Imagineers

Enabling Rightful Evolution
78
Opportunity

"There is nothing better than the encouragement of a good friend."
Katherine Hathaway

We come back to the problem of the changing possibilities - two people constantly growing from new information and their ensuing possibilities. The key is to pay attention to each other in several different ways. Pay attention to current developments while discussing how each might utilize their traits and talents to develop the "emerging person." One must remain constantly mindful of who the other person really wants to be - not just who they are, but who they want to be. Because we are constantly learning, we are also growing.

As we are growing, we are moving targets for each partner's recognition arrows. You don't enable today's person to maintain themselves as they are; you enable today's person to evolve themselves into tomorrow's person with your positive, futuristic expectations *today*. You are a force in their life and they in yours. Job One for the two of you is not "working on the relationship." Job One is working on yourself and each other. Your best efforts in your relationship will be assisting in the enabling of each other's rightful evolution.

Remember, I said to remain mindful of who the other person wants to become. The fact is, the other person may not even know themselves - nor might you. It is clear, however, that given the particular seeds of their traits and talents, beliefs and values and the sunshine of your nurture, something great and unique wants to push up through the soil of life and bloom into something special. Even if we don't know the specific application at this time for their special self, we can imagine where it might like to grow. Practice playing the available notes (recognizing and cheering their unique, wonderful behavior) as they emerge and several songs will become evident in time. As "insiders" you each share a steadily increasing confidence with the other.

Confidante
79
Technique

So here's the special role of the confidante: from your unique vantage point, while maintaining a vigilant ear and a watchful eye, you observe incoming opportunities and compare them to future possibilities. Your advantage is perspective and your goal is to tune the violin for tomorrow's song today. You cannot know the whole song as you cannot fully anticipate the future, but you can recognize the notes he will need like persistence, optimism, courage.

Each of you applauds the occurrence of those notes or acts that demonstrate the presence of those traits, reminding the other of their empowering capabilities. Your mutual goal is to germinate the talent seeds where they lie dormant, feed and water those that struggle, and maintain the ripening of the rest with your everyday sunshine. Responsibility for making these decisions rests with each person for not only their own life but for those they love.

"I once read that, in any good marriage, one partner is the gardener and the other is the garden. My husband and I take turns."
Anonymous

Your advantage is perspective and your goal is to tune the violin for tomorrow's song today.

Recognizing You
80
Strategy

I t is time to begin actively encouraging his powers of recognition for your special features. It's time you started teaching him to reciprocate. Let's show him what makes you so unique and what he can do to power it up, for both of your benefits!

> "To give and receive advice-the former with freedom and yet without bitterness, the latter with patience and without irritation-is peculiarly appropriate to genuine friendship." Cicero

It's time to turn the focus on you, to recognize your own traits and talents and communicate them. But how do you teach him to recognize your strings without sounding like a teacher? Simple - don't teach. Demonstrate. Hit him over the head with your special self. Point it out to him as it pops up in the normal course of life. I have two strategies for you to use to communicate your best self. One is to accentuate the positive. The other is to just remove all the distractions which hide the positive. And one goal: focus his attention on your essence.

If you could take that uniqueness and bottle it and wear it liberally each day it would be interesting to see which men it would attract. The next best thing to wearing it is…behaving it. It's called acting uniquely yourself. "Acting? Doesn't that require a script?" Yes.

"Where do I get my script?" It will be revealed to you as you sense opportunities to exercise your talent and apply it with your unique personality. "Where do I look for these opportunities?" Let your curiosity guide you as you go about your day. When you sense your eyes pop open you've received your cue to stop and possibility think.

> "Wisdom begins in wonder." Socrates

Okay now, remember your goal with him: focus his attention on your essence.

Accentuate the Positive
81
Strategy

L et's do the fun one first. This is the "accentuate the positive" strategy. If this one is not for you, don't panic. Everyone's personality isn't cut out for spontaneous repartee. But understand you must somehow communicate intense satisfaction in close proximity to their appearance. When you produce outstanding behavior, you should be quick to notice and compliment yourself on a job well done or a slick move cleverly executed. The more we stop to smell the flowers and point them out to others, the more wonder we experience in ourselves as well as others. Be the light of the world – make yourself shine in his eyes.

"There are always flowers for those who want to see them."
Henri Matisse

These techniques may not be your style at all. Don't fret... just cook up your own technique. The point here is that you must develop *some* technique to amplify and broadcast your everyday, spontaneous moments, as well as accentuate your positive features. Whether it's makeup for your best facial features or flattering garments for your best physical features, highlighting is an important strategy to direct his focus to your best self. No matter how you choose to accomplish it, you must *have and use* a strategy for accentuating the best features of your personality. It's when that unexpected situation confronts and challenges us that we instinctively rise to the occasion and triumph.

A wad of money falls to the ground; no one sees it but you. You call out, "Hey, excuse me but I think you've paid me too much." It's at that moment that you want to stand up and take credit, usually with a little humor to temper the pride.
This may sound like an uncomfortable exclamation, but to the one who admires you and feeds off your special traits or talents, it's nourishment. They crave it. You are feeding the hungry when you recognize yourself. They can never get enough of the real you. What an intimate moment! It's captivating and inspiring. If you don't believe me, turn it around. Don't

you thrill to his "real life" revelations? What I'm speaking here of is building a powerful magnetic force that you never turn off. You never stop reminding the other person they made the right choice. "See what makes me tick?"

After awhile you no longer need to verbally call attention to your shining moments. After awhile it's only necessary to shoot him a look or toss back your head or wink at him. He'll get the idea that you were just on stage and a little wink back would be nice. Recognition, like wrapped presents, are always welcome in any size.

Your essence is his gift and one that doesn't stop giving so long as you continue to wrap them up and present them joyfully.

See How You Are
82
Technique

Once upon a time, I had a super bartender working with me. I think it was on Wednesday nights that we were both "openers." She and I and one of the floorman would arrive early to do the set-up work. After the bar opened and customers began to trickle in more staff would begin arriving. She had a fast mind, a quick wit and a wink that left scorch marks in the minds of her unwitting targets. Underlying these were solid bartending skills and a mind that could multi-task in the middle of a major rush of customers.

This lady had a favorite phrase she'd fire at you the second she caught you exhibiting unusual behavior. I had a great time making up stuff that I would try sneaking by her, because she'd not only catch it in a heartbeat, but she'd light right up like you'd just said something that made her day, shift her tone, grin and say, "See how you are!" At first I just enjoyed the humor of it, but after a while as I observed her leveling the comment on people who truly needed an emotional boost or a behavior tune-up, I began saying it too. It was an excellent way to frame or highlight someone's behavior that best demonstrates their real character, best features and/or true talents. Try it but use it only for positive reinforcement. It's like dispensing vitamins for a growing mind.

"Knowledge of the self is the mother of all knowledge. So it is incumbent on me to know my self, to know it completely, to know its minutiae, its characteristics, its subtleties, and its very atoms."
Kahlil Gibran, "The Philosophy of Logic"

Flattery Encouraged
83
Technique

We're trained to avoid showing off or bragging about ourselves... but we do. I had never given it much thought before, but it seems the only time we're allowed to get away with flattering ourselves in public is when it's a spontaneous, emotional outbreak. After all, these gestures are just emotional, ego effervescing, as natural as a reflex hiccup and just as harmless! Take this exchange, for example with a top waitress.

Security: "You should have seen Chris last night "lose" the table of rowdies from her section with the proclamation it was free cover and amateur night at the gentleman's club on the south side of town. Ha! They just chugged their beers and had vanished by the time Cuddy and Doug showed up to move them out the door."

Chris: "Oh my gosh, you guys... I was like at the top of my game last night! I'm serious! I was smokin' hot. I was carrying three pitchers overhead in each hand and just blowing through the crowd like I was on rollerblades. Wow! Last night was awesome!"

Boasts are usually stuff people would never plan to say... and yet there's an obvious place for it. The more I heard our staff call attention in a proud yet exuberant way to their victories, the more I realized they'd created a real breakthrough for themselves. It's a wonderful method for reinforcing positive behavior - something we all need and it delighted the people who respected them. What a remarkable combination!

"The supreme happiness in life is the conviction that we are loved -
loved for ourselves, or rather, loved in spite of ourselves."
Victor Hugo

Feather Your Nest
84
Strategy

We were not individuals; we were a team. We were a crew in the hospitality business, the people business. We cared for each other. We were as one. One person's triumph was everyone's triumph, from anything as silly as being the first one to figure out how to get the new style lids off the huge maraschino cherry jars with wet hands, to being against-the-odds accurate on the cash register during a monster night in sales. One person's pride was everyone's pride. That was one benefit - feathering the group nest with bright little ribbons and bows.

Another was the immediate gratification we get from recognition after doing something well, no matter how small, from someone who cares and can relate. The more someone cares, the more gratifying the reward becomes. This in turn enhances feelings of self worth. It's a slightly different approach to the golden chain reaction. But who cares who sets the thing off as long as you just moved a little closer to a life goal or contributed a small spin to the gyroscope of your personal equilibrium.

Good news can be a wonderful thing. You never know when the other person needs to hear some, to be reassured that they are okay. With everything else that may have happened that day, you triumphed in some small or large way, and you retained your sense of joy for the event. Because they know you and love you, they must admire you. Some of their values are, therefore, alive in *you*. If you triumph *they triumph,* and their life didn't stand still today. It moved ahead because of you! Old Chinese proverbs that speak of great journeys "...presumes both traveling companions experience movement, together."

Our lives only move ahead on the backs of our triumphs. If we are attempting to travel as a team, it will be important to come along together by sharing our triumphs. Leaving our traveling companions behind on a trip is unthinkable, even if it is only one inch behind. Sometimes a day's progress only amounts to an inch. Sometimes a day's triumph only amounts to a cherry jar lid's challenge. What can it matter? If life's road is measured in miles and miles are measured in feet and feet are measured in inches, can you afford not to share that inch with a weary stranger who will share their ride with you tomorrow? Then you cannot afford to deny a ride to the one you love today. The blues occupy voids, so instead fill them with joy, no matter the portion size. A little goes a long way!

Share your triumphs! They move us forward and give us an extra helping of self worth to defray the inevitable moments that tear us down.

Robust Self Worth
85
Technique

Be assured there is a stark difference between a healthy, vibrant self image and the sick pomposity of the over-inflated egomaniac whose boasts do not compare favorably with his or her reality. Honest self appraisal is unknown to this narcissistic, self absorbed, haughty, conceited, hollow, shadow of a person. Their ability to engage in constant self inflation in the face of obvious surrounding character deficits is a sight to behold. Do not confuse people who accent their dress with the color red for the matador entirely dressed in red, who for reasons of machismo surrounds himself with bull. Check out the different types of "accenting" happening in the episodes below.

Clever and Persistent

Security (sweeping) to Opening Bartender (mopping): "Hey, did that drummer in the band eat all your fruit again? I could use an orange wedge or two or nine!"

Opening Bartender: "Yes, and you can also have a mouthful of maraschinos 'cause my clever self figured out how to get the lid off solo!"

(The previous night it took two security to get the lid off, and then they dropped the huge jar – wet fingers)

Other Bartender hearing Opening Bartender: "Ooh, I tried all Friday night. You are the "baddest" bartender in the valley!

Opening Bartender: "I am too! Ha!"

The opportunities for sharing "life's ride" with your guy are endless, but they all have one thing in common. You should always be riding proud in one of your shining traits. The bartender in this example "whipped around the block" one more time, for all of us to see in her magnificent Clever

Splendor. She got lots of ooh's and ahs too! That was an "after the fact" example but we all enjoyed it. She demonstrated that she deserves an "A" for effort. She also proved once again how clever she is.

Honesty

You to Checkout Clerk: "Excuse me, but I think you gave me the wrong change. That was a ten I gave you, not a twenty."

Checkout Clerk: "Wow, thank you!

You turning to boyfriend with a cute wink: "See how I am?"

Sensitivity

Boyfriend to you: "Hey thanks for not telling the guys at the bowling alley tonight about that great job offer you got from IBM. I know it was on your mind all night."

You (hand on his shoulder): "I knew it might make your old roommate feel a little funny because he said earlier he still hadn't heard back from them yet."

Boyfriend: "I never feel funny when I'm with you, only thrilled, See how you are!"

Pop quiz: That exchange was about a) communication, b) exhilaration, c) recognition, d) accommodation, e) admiration, f) harmony, or g) all of the above. If you said "g" *you're* the "baddest" in the valley. See how *you are*!

Guts
86
Technique

Y ou must be bold enough to stand up and be counted for what you
believe in, in front of someone you may be planning on loving, or
hey, maybe you already do. Ya gotta do it. Don't just sit around coffee
shops telling each other about your beliefs and values – point them out
when they appear in either one of you. Frame it and take or give credit for
it. He'll know when it's real, and it will reinforce his inclination to share his
special inner being with you.

This whole dating thing is really one big exam question with the entire
grade riding on, "Compare and contrast each other's values." So what do
you want him to remember? You better etch it in his brain. You want him
to see who and what you represent. You want him to recognize what makes
you special. You want him to be certain about what makes you tick so he
can figure out, anytime and anywhere, what will grow you. Remember,
you're picking out someone who is supposed to help enable you to evolve
into your best self. You'd better give your duet partner more than just a
glimpse of your strings if he's to gain an insight into your concert sound.
You better point out just which strings are responsible for which notes.

The important idea here is to shine the spotlight on your best performances
the second they happen. Who knows when that will be? Life is spontaneous,
so do what you feel and watch your cool behavior emerge! Then be ready to
take credit for it with a, "That was me!" Don't be afraid to take credit for
what makes you the special person you are.

If you fail to communicate your identity the person who is looking to find
their match may not recognize you and so... move on to someone else. Or
worse... they may mistakenly become attracted to something you're not!
Don't promote cross-eyedness in men.

"I saw the angel in the marble and carved until I set him free."
Michelangelo Buonarroti

Naked Like a Sand Bar
87
Technique

Y ou're like a person shipwrecked alone on an island when you act or look like something that doesn't mirror the real you. Thus the camouflaged you must light fires, put notes in bottles and spell out your presence in the rocks on the beach if you wish to be seen by a passing ship – guys that are your match. On the other hand, you could swim across to the sand bar where your presence would be obvious. Remove all behavior that in any way would cover up or distract another from recognizing who you really are. What behaviors might you be engaging in that would fool your rescuer?

Whatever they are, there's a very good chance you've constructed them to hide behind. We're all a little insecure. Welcome to the human race! Some are more so than others. Usually a harsh exterior indicates we're too sensitive for our environment - like the lobster. We're delicate in a hostile ocean, so we develop a hard plastic-like shell to behave around in. Or we've been abused, so we withdraw quickly like the turtle when a stranger approaches.

No matter your personal survival plan, take care to reveal your inner self when you are confident the one whose presence you share is not part of the problem but part of the solution. Musically speaking, every moment you emit classical tones when in fact you are a jazz stylist prolongs your recognition, and worse, attracts the wrong audience.

Step one: start acting and dressing like you. Let your essence be reflected in the spirit of your look and actions.

Step two: reveal your passions and your dreams once you establish trust.

What behaviors might you be engaging in that would fool your rescuer?

Section VIII

Sweet Relationships
"Great Concerts"

Game Playing
Clear Signal
Becoming
Great Karma
Harmonic Presence
Natural Attractiveness
Reflective Vision
Cosmic Coordinates
Abundance
Your Best Physical Asset
Picture It
Putting it all Together
Concert Time

HARMONY

LOVE is the child of harmony.
Harmony comes with accommodation.
Accommodation begins with recognition.
Recognition confers admiration & respect.
Admiration & respect build self confidence.
Self confidence is the engine of accomplishment.
Accomplishment is self actualizing.
Self actualization is fulfillment.
Fulfillment is harmony.
Harmony is bliss.

Game Playing
88
Technique

Here's another mistake to avoid - game playing. Recall the dialogue after bowling when you explained to your boyfriend your purpose for withholding the IBM news flash? You said, "I knew it would make your roommate feel funny." Well, just suppose you would have added, "See how much I love you?" Error...Error...Error!

That's a dangerous statement to make. Avoid it. That's a game. It might easily suggest to him that the degree of consideration he can expect to enjoy from you will be a function of the degree you love him at any point in time. Keep it simple. Stay with one message. You are good. He'll draw the immediate and obvious conclusion that he gets the benefits as long as he has you and they are only served one style, with no strings attached. If you want to tell him how much you love him, wink at him before you put your arms around him. The message will get through without the psychological weights and measures being dragged out, calibrated, compared, and factored for windage, leverage, and hidden meaning. You confuse him when you are anything but direct. It would be an indirect threat to suggest that you did it because today he qualified.

If you want to tell him how much you love him, wink at him before you put your arms around him.

Clear Signal
89
Strategy

If you are sending the wrong message, stop it. Cease your sarcasm, your timidity, your negative drama. Let the *real* you emerge. You must assume the task of the "homing device." You must emit a signal that can be easily translated by potential mates. Think about who you are. Run down the list of traits, and identify yours. (see appendices in back for lists and ideas) Go ahead and list them; you'll be impressed. Now broadcast it by living it! Dust off that timidity. You know you don't need to be a pompous fool to project and assert yourself. Cease all conflicting messages.

Think about this - You don't need to *clean up* your act... You need to *clean off* your act! Anyone who wants their message convincingly understood doesn't use sarcasm either. If you project an attitude that's not you, you risk acquiring a mate that isn't attracted to *you* but to something you invented. Remember your purpose - meeting your match. How can the one who meets you know if they match you if what you are portraying is not you? It's like telling the catalog company operator you're a size 8 instead of a size 10. You won't be happy with the relationship. It won't fit, so why distort what is! No matter how different you are, be sure your signal is clear. He's watching for you. Life's symphony is made up of many different sounds. So be yourself! Someone is your match out there. Don't hide... Vive` la difference!

If you can put a clear idea between his ears of what talents, character, personality, and values direct your existence then you will have enhanced his ability to direct his existence to accommodate yours. Hooray for you!

"I don't judge others. I say if you feel good with what you're doing,
let your freak flag fly." Sarah Jessica Parker

Becoming
90
Opportunity

"Love is friendship set to music." Anonymous

I hope I've cleared your mind and focused your sight for sharing sweet relationships with the fortunate, compatible guys out there that are just waiting to discover special, one-of-a-kind you. You are the sound of music in someone's ear and he for yours. Of course, you've made the discovery part a lot easier for him and all of the guys that are your close match by turning up the power of your unique broadcast signal.

Your personality literally radiates outward while centering yourself in a blissful state inward. You have established yourself in the universe as an intersection for harmony and love. Recognition and accommodation are becoming frequent visitors to your doorstep. You are ever watchful for opportunities to exercise your unique traits. Like checking out radio stations in a new city, it doesn't take long to pick out your favorites. The guys out there on your wave length can't help but pick up your signal. What's on your broadcast that shouldn't be on the playlist?

Confused? Go to the back of the book. Review Appendix D. In the list that profiles his grandest dream go ahead and profile yours. Open a new word document. Use the list to identify features of yours vertically. View this list as the bullet points of an outline where you develop details below each feature. This outline of your grandest dream allows your mind to "connect the dots" and generate a big picture. The big picture over the next few days will begin to morph into something that should get you excited. Once you evolve that dream a bit you will feel a lot more secure about yourself knowing what your ideal future could look like. Now compare your behavior to hers – what needs adjustment? Evolve and become thyself.

"Love is, above all, the gift of oneself."
Jean Anouilh

Great Karma
91
Opportunity

T hese recognition exercises not only broadcast a clear signal to that very special one and other guys that are a close match, but they also fill your daily life with a zesty, effervescing, positive attitude and eliminate dull tedium from giving you the blues. You also know by now - if you've been practicing - that after a relatively short time the good things in life begin to pile up and cramp your bad luck to a point where it just bogs down from all of the accommodations life has come to accumulate for you!

Some of these fortunate circumstances are the direct result of your attitude change. A few degrees change up or down can make a difference in how we are perceived by others and in turn reacted to. People mired in personal problems are often left to their own devices. People "on a roll" are often helped along by by-standers when they see they need a little push.

Thus the luck that appeared from nowhere to fix your problem is really the result of your positive attitude broadcast. People receiving the broadcast feel empowered to help you instead of threatened by one in a funk. Chances are much greater that the outsider's efforts will be appreciated and complimented than rolling the dice with someone in a gnarly mood. It's best to give them plenty of space people often reason. Their problems could rub off on you.

The higher attitude is directed to rise or the lower attitude is allowed to sink determines how you are perceived, reacted to and therefore assisted or ignored. Positive attitude is big. Equally as big is the pay-back experience of good works performed. Even those little smiles, nods, favors, thank you texts, and empowering compliments are all affecters. Overlooked snubs, ignored vengeful paybacks, forgiven transgressions and the absence of behind the back conversations you would be embarrassed to know were passed along to the subject are negative opportunities avoided. Do the math. Add positives, subtract negatives what are you left with? A much, much higher positive environment to live in which, in turn, fuels more zesty, effervescing, positive attitude. Looking for bliss? Taste life's kiss.

Harmonic Presence
92
Technique

This sort of joy can have a very debilitating effect on a negative attitude, to the point where you begin to believe yourself capable of great things. This is the courage part of harmony, and it is the beginning of the end for your life as a do nothing, go nowhere person*. It also sounds the alarm signaling a time when random fate no longer manipulates your destiny with its chaotic design. Harmonic design has stepped into the space, displacing chaos. Your resources, once activated, spoil all hope of a return to a meaningless existence. (*Some people are actually this harsh with their self appraisal – they're that anxious to graduate and/or get a mate and get a life.)

You: (after paying for the potato chips and gas at the Shop-n-Go and noting the abrupt, agitated state of your clerk) "I can't tell you how nice it is to deal with someone on the other side of the counter that knows what they're doing. Thanks for being here. I needed to see a competent person take my money for a change. I've been having one of those days."

Why did you make all that up? The clerk was obviously having a bad day but like the paramedic with a defibrillator you shocked them back into a normal heart rhythm. See how you are? Better yet, see how both of you feel now. Oh yea, it was worth it, as silly as it might seem to one with both feet on the ground. If you died 2 seconds later you would have left the world a better place! The news that night would have quoted the clerk's remembrance of how you had touched her. Now the world was touched! See how it can be? Your last broadcast would have been huge!

"No act of kindness, no matter how small, is ever wasted." Aesop

Natural Attractiveness
93
Opportunity

C ommunication comes from example. He will recognize your essence by your behavior. Guys that are a match looking for grand adventure are sure to find you permanently irresistible. Your ability to be attractive no longer relies on your flair for applying makeup at a stop light, propelling witty, well-timed punch lines at the coffee shop or quoting sports statistics at the drop of a gym bag. Once you spring from that limb of everyday tedium into the fresh air of life's possibilities, you'll discover the power in your unique combination of traits and talents to propel yourself upward, never again to return to earth.

That's *natural attraction.* And that unique combination unlocks a unique lock – his! So don't be wasting your time with guys that "don't get it," "haven't got a clue," or are just plain "out to lunch." They were meant not to, but others are. So keep the faith, exercise patience with those that don't fit and *stay available* for those that do! Among those that do is one that is a *perfect* fit! Now let's get back to your power and the keys you hold for setting up the force-field that will loudly broadcast your unique signal.

Your ability to be attractive no longer relies on your flair for applying makeup at a stop light, propelling witty, well-timed punch lines at the coffee shop or quoting sports statistics at the drop of a gym bag.

Reflective Vision
94
Opportunity

From little bitty spontaneous acts of courtesy that tickle their fancy, to earthshaking deeds that boggle your mind, you practice using your *reflective* vision. Like your reflection in the mirror, you project another person's situation onto yourself and then ask what you would do for yourself in those circumstances. This is the vision that looks at another and sees what you could do to help make their minute or even their day. You're not waiting for a flood or a forest fire to see that another person could use a hand; you're looking for subtle opportunities. You are a nurturer. Sometimes opportunities require a little courage, so courage exercises are good. The more you use your nerve, the easier it becomes. You soon learn fear is a false prophet. Nothing but joy results from sending out joy and simple goodwill to others.

Amy: "Excuse me, I see your children have you at your wit's end, and it's going to be a little while before our plane boards. See, I'm a college student majoring in Child Development, and we had to write a children's story where each of the children move their hands or wiggle their fingers at certain times during the telling of the story. If it's okay with you, I think I can occupy their time, use up some of that energy and entertain us all for a few minutes. Here's my college picture I.D. My name is Amy and I go to State."

Mother: "Oh, you must be an angel, Amy! I'm sure they'd love it."

❖ You have established yourself in the universe as an intersection for harmony and love.

❖ A person once armed with knowledge of the natural power they possess to foster and nurture their own as well as another's fulfillment …becomes *a formidable ally* in life's grand adventure.

Cosmic Coordinates
95
Opportunity

When you plan to move to action, you've planned to exercise and experience your essence. Your essence is a beautiful, powerful thing. When you exercise your first deed to lift another, you've moved your wings to lift yourself. The more you exercise your wings, the stronger they become. Someday soon you'll pinch yourself and realize you're not ten feet tall at all; you'll realize you're flying! A time will come when flight will be second nature to you. Your thoughts will naturally soar to the possibilities as you scan the horizon and achieve your dreams.

> ❖ You'll come to discover that life's true riches reside in the thrill of the heart as the soul soars to its challenge and accomplishes its mission.

The whole universe is engaged in the harmonic act of accommodating its evolution. Isn't it about time you got in sync with the main program and experienced the thrill of being a player instead of a spectator in the part that was reserved just for you? Is this excitement or what?!

> ❖ Your mission is to thrill to the challenge of your unique potential by actually engaging it.

Only you can imagine it. Only you can experience it. Only you can engage it. Like sitting behind the wheel, you lift your hand to the gear shift and engage the forward gear. Like picking up the bow and contacting your own strings, fulfilling your potential is a grand adventure that doesn't happen by coincidence. You must *plan* the experiences of your life to utilize your potential.

> ❖ You must plan your experience to experience your plan.

"None of us knows what the next change is going to be, what unexpected opportunity is just around the corner, waiting a few months or a few years to change all the tenor of our lives."
Kathleen Norris

Abundance
96
Opportunity

L ife provides abundant opportunities to apply your resources and
advance your evolution as well as that of others. You must learn to see
them. You must sharpen your vision and develop good judgment. The more
practiced your vision, the more opportunities you will recognize. The more
often you act on what you recognize to be obvious opportunities to advance
the growth of others, the faster you advance yourself. The more contact you
have with those you advance, the more your relationships advance. Close
relationships advance the fastest where each helps empower the other to
reach their goals. The opportunities are the lock; your action to jump in and
do something with those opportunities is the key. You must plan to act on
opportunities. Commit to action - that is your pledge! Just go for it!
Harmony never sleeps. Flowers await their sunshine. The strings await the
bow, and love awaits you. The endorphins released will make you a believer!

Remember Amy at the airport a minute ago? She was familiar with working
with children, yet out of her element in a public place with people she
didn't know. The situation was negative in that the children were nearly out
of control and distracting to the other passengers. The person Amy wanted
to approach was tense and obviously frazzled from a long day. It would be
easy to see that the woman could turn on Amy to take out her frustrations.
Amy took a chance. opportunity knocked, and Amy answered the call
because her unique skills were a perfect fit and she knew it. She took a
chance and came out with a hero's welcome. You know she felt sky high
when she walked on that plane! Natural euphoria is a sweet buzz and
happily addictive too.

"Creativity comes from trust. Trust your instincts.
And never hope more than you work." Rita Mae Brown

Hey, I'm not asking you to do stuff that turns you off. That isn't you; it's just the opposite. I'm suggesting you do what *will* turn you on. Do stuff that is you – uniquely you. In fact, by taking a moment when opportunity knocks (or sometimes just tickles) to look at what is beckoning, you may find multiple traits and talents wanting to participate. You therefore are capable of sounds that are not really the product of just one string or talent, but when combined with others really create a synergy to produce a third sound or act. It's called music. It's called *loving*.

So get ready to amaze yourself with the very cool combinations that result when you attempt to enable or empower another. You'll always entertain and actualize yourself by contributing your essence to another's need.

"The doors we open and close each day decide the lives we live."
Flora Whittemore

Your Best Physical Asset
97
Opportunity

Over the weeks and months the good stuff you generate by accommodating others piles up and reaches critical mass. It begins breeding good luck all by itself. Certain Eastern religions refer to good karma as the result of behavior in past incarnations or lives. I see it affecting the current life. A sure sign of being overtaken by good karma is short term facial muscle fatigue triggered by compulsive grinning. The good stuff starts happening and you start smiling. As your "luck" continues (which is actually your *harmonious* behavior paying dividends) you'll soon find these facial muscles will acquire such tone that they'll radiate a natural, effortless smile all by themselves. It's smiling without trying!

Configuring one's face in a smile evokes a positive, immediate mood change. Try it. You'll be surprised at how it will change your attitude. In telemarketing one is taught to smile over the phone to change the dynamic of the conversation. A smile is a powerful asset. Deploy it often!

While traveling in France and Italy I learned to approach the locals with a broad smile, and a long pause - still smiling broadly, before acting-out my question. I was always treated wonderfully even though I couldn't speak a sentence in either language. The smile always translated. The details I handled with pantomime. They were always amused and ...accommodated me. I had "recognized" them with my smile, patience and silly body language. It even works on strangers in this country! But then you knew that. Well a lot of people don't – I'd say the majority haven't a clue. No matter what, lead off with a big smile then pause, then deliver your thought. It will tell them you're not hostile or afraid and you'll be easy to deal with. Works like a charm!

Do it often and you'll have reason to do it even more! Just walk along, make a smile, and hold it until it starts to feel uncomfortable. Relax, and do it again. Pick out a landmark on your way to a certain class and whenever you see it smile your most exaggerated smile and hold it until your face cracks!

(Building muscle: no pain, no gain.) If someone notices you, crank it up a little higher for them and watch them respond with a smile. In no time you'll smile without any effort and your face will just light up for the slightest reasons. Remember, untrained smile muscles don't respond to subtle cues, but exercised ones will. Looking good is all about being attractive, and nothing attracts people of both sexes more than a pleasantly charged face that produces a beautiful smile - effortlessly! Smile, it will make you feel better. Your front teeth could use some air.

No matter what, lead off with a big smile then pause, then deliver your thought.

Your Best Physical Asset Is Your Smile ☺

Picture It
98
Opportunity

B efore you do something important, you often picture it first. You imagine how it might be in reality. You project the scene with your mind's eye. You do this to learn how you will like something before you spend the capital to achieve it. You want to look great at the party. You know the feeling you're trying to achieve, so you picture yourself in different outfits, hair styles, makeup and jewelry to sense how you'll feel. While admittedly it's a mental thing, it comes pretty close to reality if you spend some quality time filling in the details of the picture. Once you're satisfied that all the pieces are accounted for and nothing's been left to chance, you begin to model the fit and the feel of it. Your facility of picturing or creating model scenes in your mind of *what it might be like* is exactly the technique you'll respond with when your curiosity sounds the alarm and opportunity tempts you to action.

"Deeds of kindness are equal in weight to all the commandments."
Talmud, Rabbinical writings.

At the airport, Amy saw the children and the chaos and was taken with the idea to replicate a scene from school. She used her power to visualize herself with these children: where she would sit to tell the story, how much time she would have before the plane would board, how she would approach their mother. She worked the idea around in her mind a few different ways. She realized she could use some of her Theater minor to really turn-up the drama and grab their attention. And hold it.

By the time she moved to action, rising from her seat to approach their mother, she had rehearsed the scene already several times in her mind, even how she would react smoothly if the mother barked at her. It took courage, but "picturing it" gave her the confidence to go for it.

"Happiness does not consist in pastimes and amusements
but in virtuous activities."
Aristotle

Putting it all Together
99
Strategy

M usic only comes with practice.

- ❖ Get to know your instrument.
- ❖ Practice tuning the strings.
- ❖ Practice playing the notes.

Practice playing the notes... that make the music that your tuned instrument plays best.

- ❖ Practice using the techniques.

Practice using the techniques... that play the combinations of notes... that make the music... that your tuned instrument plays best.

- ❖ Regularly exercise the muscles.

Regularly exercise the muscles... that control the techniques... that play the combination of notes... that make the music... that your tuned instrument plays best.

- ❖ Practice playing the songs.

Practice playing the songs... that exercise the muscles, that control the techniques, that play the combination of notes, that make the music, that your tuned instrument plays best.

- ❖ That's what you do for you.
- ❖ That's what you do for him.
- ❖ That's what you teach him to do for you.
- ❖ That's what you do for each other.

Concert Time
100
Strategy

T he concert of your life is a balanced combination of solos and duets. Solos satisfy individual needs; duets satisfy mutual needs. By pacing your performance to stay in sync with him and he with you, you ensure that you'll both be playing the same songs together. Some thoughts on your future together might include:

- ❖ He must *share* your vision of a Concert.
- ❖ His eye for *detail* must mirror yours.
- ❖ You must *want* to accommodate each other.
- ❖ Your mutual enthusiasm must *exceed* the challenge.
- ❖ You must *respect* each other.

"He must *share* your vision of a Concert" means that you've actively talked about each other's special features and the possibilities for coordinating their application and development. He recognizes and accepts the wonderful potential such a mutual effort could hold for both of your futures. He understands that nature holds an expectation for each of you as individuals to apply your talents and contribute to humankind's evolution. He agrees you both should move ahead together like to two legs moving a body up a mountain. He believes that by constant encouragement and optimism, a concerted effort will achieve not only your mutual fulfillments but your day to day happiness. He understands the concept and endorses it through his behavior. He is enthusiastic to support, coach, sponsor, and enable your evolution, understanding the effects such behavior will have on your relationship with him.

"His eye for *detail* must mirror yours" means that he has come to recognize the special features of your personality, as well as your recognition for his. He shares your interest in focusing the conversations from time to time on the intricate particulars that define each of your traits and talents. He enjoys these conversations and agrees on their importance. His appreciation for planning their application is obvious and enthusiastic. He is committed to their refinement. His vision agrees with yours in all aspects important to you. His concept of an enabling relationship matches yours. His vision and your vision match your mutual priorities. The future's so bright, you gotta wear shades!

"You must *want* to accommodate each other" means that you are willing to take turns stepping aside or pitching in when the other's progress would be helped. It means recognizing the necessity of constantly enabling the other to move ahead if one is to expect assistance themselves. It means alternating the individual priorities so that equality of progress is assured. It means taking turns being the ladder so the other can do the climbing and so that both can reach the goal. It means pointing out unique opportunities that conflict with one's own plans. It means being admired and respected as a helpmate. It means giving in order to receive; exercising patience when you'd prefer to exercise privilege; sharing a ride at every opportunity and alternating when two can't ride together. It means taking turns enabling each other. It means sharing the happiness while promoting harmony because the vision of your dream motivates you.

Yes, you bothered to take the time to imagine a very attractive set of circumstances and now you feel like it's within the realm of possibility. Therefore your dream is not a fantasy, it is your goal.

"By learning to contact, listen to, and act on our intuition, we can directly connect to the higher power of the universe and allow it to be our guiding force." Shakti Gawain

"Your mutual enthusiasm must *exceed* the challenge." This means that you must calculate, as best you can, what the two of you are attempting to accomplish in a lifetime and compare it to your mutual will. Have you known him long enough to have personally witnessed his resourcefulness, persistence, drive, ambition, patience, stamina, flexibility, courage and determination to carry out his end of the bargain? Are you honest in the appraisal of your own capabilities? Have you, on the other hand, perhaps underrated the synergistic effect of two people generating an abundance of enthusiasm from planning their work and working their plan? Calculating whether your mutual enthusiasm is up to the challenge is hardly a scientific exercise. It is rather a consciously asked question that can be expected to elicit an unconscious "hunch" or feeling. Your intuition becomes your guide in this matter. Prayer can be an efficient messenger should your intuition fail you. Don't believe in prayer? Here's your chance. Go to a quiet place, close your eyes, clear your mind (may take a few minutes), ask your question, and listen to your inner voice deliver your provider's thoughts. It's a handy resource, 24/7.

> "In prayer, more is accomplished by listening than by talking."
> Jane Francis De Chantal.

"You must respect each other" means that you have identified, measured, quantified, qualified, and examined each other's beliefs and values and find them to be on balance, fair and reasonable. Your admiration and respect function on what you understand to be motivating and controlling the acts of the other person. You may not agree with an act on occasion, but you should agree with the beliefs and values that sponsored them. Admiration and respect fuel desire. The motivation to "ride together" ceases when the fuel dries up. Be sure to maintain the fuel source. You must respect each other. It's not just a song; it's a concert! It's not just your life; it's your dream! Consider yourself capable of amazing results.

Finally

Good Luck in your quest for finding, winning, and holding on to that very special guy out there who's just waiting to discover you. Guys love being discoverers! Remember that luck is nothing more than preparation meeting opportunity. Opportunities abound and are free for the taking. Preparation, on the other hand, must be planned, practiced, polished and produced. Your preparation begins with opening your eyes to your special traits and talents. Recognizing the power nature has equipped you with and employing it to enable others prepares you. People are attempting to progress in life all around you. Recognizing opportunities to help, whether big or small, sustain you by the reactions they cause when you bring yourself to action. With sufficient empowering behavior, your spirit will soar above the crowds, the chaos and the confusion, and your bliss is assured.

> Prepare to make music - Pick up a bow.
> Prepare for a song - Put on a grin.

Prepare to sync with nature - Put on a smile.
Prepare for bliss ...A delicious rendezvous awaits you.

Now the angels know that you know the secret of the universe: how harmony is created. They'll be arranging things for you, so don't be surprised how easy and fun it will be. Where will you begin? See appendices in back for lists and ideas. Use one to inventory your personality. Look at who you are. You will identify your wonderful talents and character strengths. Think about it like this person (you) is your twin and they could use your perspective. They would like your ideas on their highest and best use in society. What could they excel at? Don't know? Okay, expressed another way, what would they love to do more than anything else? Don't hold back. "Use plenty of marble." There will be plenty of time to remove the excess later. Remember Michelangelo's strategy...

"I saw the angel in the marble and carved until I set him free."

Now take that essence that is your "sister" and wave a magic wand over it and imagine just how amazing a life she could have once she began to visualize the details of it and was motivated to move to the next step she would need to take on that fantastic journey to her, rather – your dreams.

Next you will begin practicing your recognition skills, developing deep vision "nightclub eyes." With practice you will be ready to begin artfully interviewing the men your angels will begin providing for your examination. Make sure they share your beliefs and values. Some will be just for practice but which ones?

❖ Remember that list of traits (in back) awaits your self appraisal.
❖ Recognize how wonderful thou art!
❖ Practice recognizing and nurturing the flower that wants to grow inside you.
❖ He'll likely need an experienced gardener with nightclub eyes!
❖ Better include a great cheerleader and coach too...

He needs all the help you can give him – cheering and coaching, your game! Is that a campus strategy you can live with? You got game now girl!

Practice recognizing and nurturing the flower that wants to grow inside you.

Glossary

Accommodation: supplying some or all of the assistance one needs in order that they may accomplish a goal – however minor it appears to us. Friends make room in their heads for their friend's eccentricities, strange opinions, differing philosophies, nutty mannerisms, and peculiar eating and dressing habits. Tolerance is a tool accommodators learn to use. If you can't support it, ignore it. (Unless health or safety is at risk)

Actualize: Becoming the person you are ideally capable of being.

Affectations: Exhibiting a manner of behavior fabricated to impress those viewing us. You spend the weekend in Atlanta and now are speaking with a southern accent 3 weeks after your return.

Animal Magnetism: Sexual attraction.

Behavior Modification: The study or act of changing a person or animal's usual reaction to a situation or specific stimuli. Raising your eyebrows dramatically causes your pet to expect a treat and therefore sit up in anticipation. Enough repetitions of placing the pet in the sit-up positions while raising your eyebrows *and* supplying the treat cause the pet to modify its behavior on your eyebrow cue.

Beliefs & Feelings: Our collected personal opinions or values and how we emotional react to what we perceive or believe we perceive. Our opinions color our perceptions, especially vividly when emotion is present or is activated. Beliefs and feelings attempt to guide behavior. Anxiety results when we choose to act in conflict with what we believe and feel is appropriate. Often people from similar backgrounds share similar beliefs/ values and feelings, and therefore find relations with each other easier than those from backgrounds with *possibly* dissimilar beliefs and feelings.

Body Chemistry: The body has its own "medicine cabinet" and, depending on what we believe is happening, glands and organs in the body react with chemicals to serve the purpose and facilitate our needs. Emergencies, for instance, strengthen our muscles, and concentrate our power to focus. The term also can refer to like mindedness and similar energy levels.

Body Language: Positioning and moving the body and its parts in reaction to what is being thought. Often these are unconscious reactions. Skilled observers may be able to interpret what we are really thinking by viewing our behavior. A hand to the nose sometimes signals a mistruth being told or an unsavory thought being contemplated.

Chain Reaction: Reactions that seem to get a life of their own and prompt other actions, which in turn prompt more actions. Set up a series of objects that will fall into the next, one after the other, all started by a single action. Enter the realm of unintended consequences!

Charisma: The uncanny natural attraction some people generate. It is typically personality driven.

Comfort Zone: A situation that feels good. In your room with a favorite album playing perhaps, or together with a person with similar beliefs and values who lets you relax and just be yourself.

Commitment: To assure another of a course of action.

Confidante: One entrusted with another's confidential information.

Core Essentials: The defining elements of one's personality: courage, honesty, respect, humor, energy, resourcefulness, optimism, etc.

Cosmic Coordinates: When serving the greatest good relative to your unique combination of personality, talent and skill sets; whenever your essence is concentrated producing your best beneficial, unique, contribution. It might be said that you are currently at the intersection of your potential & opportunity.

Critical Mass: The point at which circumstances change, physical properties take on a new definition, our opinion alters, coincidence can no longer be ignored. Enough couples finally get on the dance floor that you feel like you won't be "the only people out there." Enough couples on the dance floor and the weight carrying characteristics are exceeded and the floor begins to collapse. Critical mass was achieved, figuratively speaking, in the first and actually in the last. When enough is enough, good or bad.

Cross Pollinate: An action serves to create a reaction which then reactively returns the favor to serve the server…a favor returned, so to speak.

Decode: The process the brain uses to convert incoming sounds, sights, smells, feelings, tastes into its own bio-chemical meaning.

De Rigueur: French for socially obligatory – a must do, like wearing a gown to the prom.

Defense Mechanisms: Our body comes equipped with certain automatic responses that serve to maintain its good health and happiness. Eyes blink when something comes too near to them. Memory suspends when awful events exceeds its limits to process the event. Glands secrete hormones to assist the body's capabilities to overcome the threat.

Dreams: Here to mean imagined ideal future circumstances, regarding careers, family life. Not unconscious, sleep induced dreams.

Dynamic Nature: The ability of a person to change their focus, attitude and energy to rise to the occasion with little or no preparation – on the spur of the moment. To move from assorted different tasks marshalling their enthusiasm and energy to meet the goal.

Empower: To provide or activate resources for achievement.

Enable: Help another accomplish. Not used here in the negative, i.e. to prevent another to escape their addiction or harmful behavior by supplying a necessary, negative resource(s) like money, drugs or shelter.

Encode: The process the brain uses to translate its ideas into meaningful communication so others may know what we are thinking – like speech and or body language.

Endorphin: Hormones that bind to opiate receptors reducing pain and increasing pleasure. A fuel for behavior modification.

Euphoria: The feeling of happiness, joy, bliss, well being.

Evolve: The transition from who we are to who we will become. Becoming.

Extroversion: An "extrovert." A personality said to be outgoing. Tending to reach out to others, interact with them, and communicate freely with minimal reservations. Relaxed in a group.

Facilitator: One who assists or encourages another or others to accomplish their task. Often support groups have a person who starts the meeting by explaining the rules and goals of the group, ensures everyone participates appropriately within the time limits, and closes the meeting.

Golden Rule: "Do onto others as you would have them do onto you." An axiom repeated in most religions.

Harmony: To interact in a fashion that maintains and encourages the individuality of each without harmful expense to any.

Harmonic Presence: A blissful state, present for perhaps no other reason than by the absence of conflict, chaos, or confusion.

Hidden Agenda: A purpose other than the one stated or expected that may drive the outcome and redirect the activity and purpose.

Highest & Best Use: Assuming a role that would have us best utilizing the current resources as well as our own talents and experience to facilitate everyone's purposes, not just our own.

Hormones: Chemicals our bodies produce that act like a loudspeaker issuing a call to action to specific cells as they flow throughout the body. Hormones essentially reconfigure the body for a specific use by activating and/or deactivating specific cells that pertain to that purpose.

Intimate: Confidential, private as opposed to public information or behavior, typically kept private and limited to sharing with only trusted individuals. See Confidante. May also refer to physical or sexual.

Introversion: An "introvert." Someone preferring privacy and likely uncomfortable in a group.

Law of Unintended Consequences: An imagined rule asserting the likelihood that not all results will be favorable, let alone be correctly anticipated. The unbalanced wash machine pounds the wall that in turn shakes the topless jug of detergent loose from its perch above, causing it to empty a few ounces of its syrupy liquid onto the full basket waiting for the dryer. Who could have guessed you'd be washing a few items twice!

Leap of Faith: Exercising nerve held in reserve for those moments when circumstances don't support the belief that the goal about to be attempted can be actually realized. Failure appears more imminent. Notwithstanding, you go for it anyway. Your hope being that you will rise above it.

Life Plan: A person or couple's envisioned goals describing in detail how and why they will live their lives over its entirety and updated frequently.

Love: To experience a strong emotional kinship, attraction, affection, and dedication to another. See Index.

Metaphor: Reducing an object or opportunity to a concept to help explain something usually quite unlike it but sharing remarkable parallels. Child birth might be seen as a metaphor for graduation helping to explain how happiness and emotional distress mark the start of a new beginning in life with all its ripple effects on relationships, dress, behavior, expectations and experimentation - very different occasions, yet uncannily parallel in ways. The violin has provided many interesting metaphorical parallels for us.

Mission Statement: Primary purposes of group or organization.

Opiate: A drug; in this case, a hormone having narcotic qualities.

Persona: The projected appearance one wishes the public to view, as opposed to what actually is being felt by the person.

Possibility Thinking: An approach to one's circumstances, predicament or general philosophy that suggests one first look to what might be as opposed to what is or has happened. Taking stock of one's skill-set and resources at every turn and especially when fate deals us the crisis card. Setting emotion aside no matter the devastation or calamity to learn what can be salvaged, found, refashioned or invented to put us back on our track to fulfillment.

Preventive Maintenance: Attending to minor issues on a regular basis before they become major problems.

Provider-Protector: The traditional male role model in most societies, pre mid-twentieth century. Provide food as hunter and protection from attack. The traditional woman's role is described as Mother-Nurturer.

Punk'd: Create a scenario that attempts to fool the target person or people into believing they are in a crisis, and then aggravate it to a point of maximum tension before unveiling the plot and releasing the emotionally wrought to a state of relief and laughter to entertain all – hopefully.

Recognition: Appreciation,   approval,   affirmation,   awareness, authentication, applause, respect, valuation, credit. Our blasting cap.

Reflective Vision: Reverse your perspective. Put yourself in another person's shoes; seeing and feeling what it is like to be them. Now bring your skill set and presence to their aid. How would I help myself right now if I were in their situation, knowing what I know – from my perspective?

Reflex Action: Behavior in response to action. Unconscious reaction to a stimulus. Doctor pops your knee with a rubber mallet and ....

Reinforcement: To encourage a habit or response to a specific stimulus. Training uses reinforcement, usually repetitious a reward, to set a specific expectation – getting the reward, to be anticipated as the direct result of the cue or stimuli. The customer raises her glass and the bartender stops what she's doing to make another cocktail and serve it quickly. The customer paying cash with $5 for the $2.75 drink leaves the change as the tip. Bartender and other service workers quickly learn to respond promptly to good tippers since their hourly pay is usually low and their income depends on what they make directly from their patron's tips. To Insure Prompt Service – TIPS.

Role Play: To behave in the manner of a person performing a particular occupation or task for purpose of instruction. "Okay, so everyone understands how to properly react to a table of rowdy cowboys in town for the rodeo. Let's have Juanita be the waitress and Tom and I will be the cowboys giving her a hard time. Cuddy will be the manager. Let's see how

Juanita goes immediately on defense for the cowboys when Cuddy asks if everything is all right to her at their table. They, sensing her 'take a bullet' for them, immediately settle down and become model good old boys, still having a great time. Okay Juanita, approach our table and let's act it out."

Screening: Selection based on specific criteria.

Self Actualize: See *actualize*.

Skill Set: The collection of talents, strategies, techniques, motor skills and know-how one uses to carry out a task.

Stimulus: An action that may provoke a reaction.

String Set: A metaphor for a person's talent, skills, personality, and virtues that combine to complete the picture of the individual. Instincts, intuitions, and experiences are present just behind the curtain influencing the actor as well.

Sunshine: That helping, caring, encouraging, facilitating behavior that broadcasts beyond the intended receiver to attract the attention and admiration of others.

Synergy: A magical alliance where actions and reactions occur to create a multiplication instead of an addition with each other. One child + one baby-sitter = two. Three babysitters + one child = four. However, One babysitter + three children = Five. Again, one task + one talent = accomplishment. However, two talents + one task = art.

Talent: Propensity to excel at a particular endeavor. An aptitude, flair, genius, capability for accomplishing that which would challenge the average person to a point of frustration or failure.

Temporary Infatuation: A very strong but passing interest in another.

TIVO: The television recorder that allows programs to be selected in advance and recorded automatically. It also allows live as well as recorded programs to be stopped, slow motioned, and fast forwarded.

Traits: Used here, personality features like energetic, quiet, caring, boisterous, bold. See the list in Appendix B.

Trial & Error: A system of learning through trying and failing, eliminating flawed possibilities to eventually come to a "best" solution. Edison failed thousands of times eliminating possibilities while accumulating knowledge of the subject to finally produce the light bulb and a series of amazing machines, the record player being one, mother of the CD player.

Try-Out Dates: A clever method for minimizing one's exposure to initial possible badly ending dates by hooking up with friends later in the evening. By decreasing the one on one length of time exposed, one dilutes exposure to potential jerks and gains a different perspective of the guy's behavior by adding friends to the mix. Now there's three of you to critique him later.

Unconscious mind: The wonderful mental faculty at everyone's disposal (it's free) that's great for lots of stuff – like doing research and producing hunches. Thinking that occurs without our awareness.

Validate: To confirm, affirm, authenticate. Used here it means to communicate to him that his role is romantic and not furniture mover.

Virtues: That which makes people and animals delightful. Courage is first because it empowers the rest. It gives one the power to enforce under great duress the others, like honesty and fidelity.

Vision: The ability to look into what might be and describe the details. Imagination is "key" to vision. Imagining yourself in the future at your highest and best use gives your unconscious mind a destination to navigate your behavior toward. Hunches and intuition guide your path. Curiosity pulls you forward into the unknown. The farther you travel your blissful life path the more you become empowered to continue. The primary task of your partner is to encourage that voyage... and share the chores.

War Story: Very challenging personal experience. Reveals character traits. May contain distortions, exaggerations and lack objectivity.

Whisper Power: The knack of creating a vacuum in the listener's ear for your message.

Appendix A: The Prospect's Interview

Fill in the blanks: How much background does he share with you? Any one of these answers could prompt your curiosity to ask more about this part of him. Stay casual but focused. Share your background but keep your stories brief.

Home and Parents
    Farm Raised____ Like__ Disliked __
    Small town____ Like__ Disliked __
    Big City ____ Like__ Disliked __
    Only Child__ Like__ Disliked __
    Brothers__ Like__ Disliked __   Sisters__ Like__ Disliked __
        He's the Oldest__, Youngest__, Middle__
    Parents
        Two__ One__
        Likes Father __ Dislikes __
        Likes Mother __ Dislikes __
    Step Parents
        Two __ One __
        Likes Step Father __ Dislikes __
        Likes Step Mother __ Dislikes __
    Both Work __   Mom/Step Mom Stays at Home__
Mom/Step Mom works____
        Dad/Step Dad works Dad/Step Dad stays at Home

Traditional School __or Home Schooled__
    Liked School__ Disliked School __
    Grades Good __ Great__ Just Passing__
    Involved in Sports__ Clubs__ Activities__
Church
    Attended__ Attends___
    Believer__ Strong __ Medium___ Not at All __

Career

        Major_____

        Minor_____

        Not Declared_____

        No Idea_____

Artist____ Scientist_____ Introvert____ Extrovert____ Team Player ___
Lone Operative ____

Essay: How does his passion & character compare to yours? General questions:

"Todd, If you won the million dollar lottery how would it change the next 12 months of your life?"

"Ok Todd, and then what would the next year likely be like?   Or…

"So John, what sorts of things get you the most excited – like what you're really good at or really get turned on with – sports, academics…what's your thing – your wicked hot passion?"

"Oh really, so recall for me a situation, John, where you thought you were going to crash and burn and you somehow turned it around and triumphed in spite of the odds. You were like, amazing!"

Do the answers talk about others or just him. Is he helping or hoarding. Is he mature or adolescent-like. Is he imaginative or without ideas of his own. Is he complacent or have a fire for life in his belly. Is he a winner or a loser? Are you buying what this guy is selling? Will your best friends like him? Will he like your best friends? Would you trust him to take care of your pet for a week?

Take a moment and note here what else you are wondering.

Appendix B: Rate Your Prospect
Character –Talents - Personality

	1	2	3	4	5
Achiever					
Ambition					
Articulate					
Bully					
Cheap					
Creative					
Compassion					
Confusing					
Courage					
Curiosity					
Cuteness					
Courtesy					
Dependability					
Determination					
Dominating					
Drinker					
Drive					
Egotism					
Empathy					
Energy					
Evasive					
Excessive					
Extravagant					
Fair Play					
Flirty					
Funny					
Good Will					
Goofy					
Happy					

	1	2	3	4	5
Helper					
Honesty					
Hot Tempered					
Humility					
Humor					
Integrity					
Intelligence					
Intimidating					
Kind					
Loud/Quiet					
Manners					
Maturity					
Morality					
Opinionated					
Optimism					
Passionate					
Patience					
Persistence					
Possibility Thinking					
Positive Attitude					
Resourcefulness					
Self Esteem					
Sensitivity					
Silly					
Smoker					
Snobbery					
Submissive					
Talented					
Teaser					
Timid					
Underachiever					
Wimpish					
Wise					

Appendix C: Event Journal

"Sharing the Stage"

Memorable events should be journaled. They are the seasoning in your life, good or bad. Later you may see it all as good. Time provides experience which should give you a broader perspective. In any event, let your memory for details be noted here and be sure to date each event with this guy. You will be surprised at what you learn by reading it back to yourself in as little as a week and certainly a month. Monitor your feelings, understand where this is going.

	Great	Good	Crummy
Date			
Time			
Place			
Event			
Holiday			
Weekend			
Weekday			
First Coffee at			
Second Coffee at			
First Date at			
Second Date at			
Double date whoelse			
I think I'm in luv			
I think I'm in trouble			
I think I hate him			
I think he likes me			
I think he's a horn dog			
I think he really thinks I'm hot!			
I think he's hot			

What Happened….write as vividly as the event requires.
Caution your grandchildren may read this.

He did

I did

He said

I said

He laughed

I laughed

I wish I would…

I wish he would …

So today he learned this about me or my dreams (goals)

So here's what I learned about him or his dreams

If a dream, what would the next mini-step be to helping him or me attain it?

How do I feel about asking or telling him?

General Observation about us:

Appendix D:
Three Things You Must Learn About Him

Jot down his favorite story, his grandest dream, and his best role model. What will you learn about him that will later prove to help immensely if you take down some quick notes now, while they're vivid?

Example: You just came back from your second coffee shop meeting with him and now's the time to record it.

Imagine now its seven weeks later. You've really got some mixed feelings and you'd love to resolve them. Go to these notes. There may be revelations waiting for you here. One will be perspective. You will recall your enthusiasm and quickly compare it to now, _____ weeks later. It will be worth the time now if you're on the fence about him later.

Open a new document on your PC and title it Chem Notes or whatever class you took last semester just in case somebody peaks. Code his name in case somebody does a search or just print it out then delete the .doc lest a goblin put it on the net…eeeck!

His Favorite Story: Profile it
His Favorite Story: Write it down

His Grandest Dream: Profile it,
His Grandest Dream: Write it down

His Best Role Model: Profile it
His Best Role Model: Write it down

His Favorite Story: Profile it

Happy or sad?

Fun or not?

Day or night?

Life threatening?

Super high energy?

Within the law/not?

Complex or simple?

How scared was he?

Was respect involved?

How was his self esteem affected?

Is the story believable?

How much did he exaggerate?

Does the story have any heroes?

Any villains?

Is his family central to it?

What level of enthusiasm does it show?

How deeply passionate is he?

Is anger, revenge, ill will involved?

How seriously was he tested?

Is the telling of it emphasize the conflict or the resolution?

Is his emphasis on the pain he went through or the joy of coming through it?

Is the theme about winning against all odds?

Does he gain something grand or suffer a major loss?

Is he clearly glad it happened because he learned, because he survived, simply because he won, because someone else was helped, or because it was a thrill. Did revenge play a key role?

His Favorite Story: Write it down

His Grandest Dream: Profile it

Fun or not?

Super high energy?

Complex or simple?

How much respect will he have then?

How passionate is he about it?

How passionate is he normally?

Does it involve moving.?

Moving frequently?

Is the dream wildly achievable or totally ridiculous?

Will it take long to achieve?

What special preparations is he planning?

How realistic or fantastic is it?

Is his family central to it?

What level of enthusiasm does he show?

How deeply passionate is he?

Will it make him rich?

How about famous?

How about happy?

How about contented?

Will it be fun getting there?

Will it be draining?

Will the kids see their father?

Will it be stressful getting there?.

Will it be stressful being there?

His Grandest Dream: Record it

His Best Role Model: Profile Him

His Father?
Sports hero?
Athletic
Movie star
Soldier
Businessman
Family man
Character in fiction
Super Hero
Smart
Rich
Brave
Handsome
Manly
Competitor
Achiever
Leader
Team player
Spiritual
Religeous

How does he compare to the role model?

Is he really trying to copy him?

Does he study the person?

Is it the emotional, mental, physical, or all that he admires in his role model?

What doesn't he care for in him?

His Best Role Model: Write about it.

Appendix E: Quotes by Famous People

"Admiration is a very short-lived passion that immediately decays upon growing familiar with its object, unless it be still fed with fresh discoveries, and kept alive by a new perpetual succession of miracles rising up to its view." Joseph Addison

"No act of kindness, no matter how small, is ever wasted." Aesop

"Without passion man is a mere latent force and possibility, like the flint which awaits the shock of the iron before it can give forth its spark."
Henri Frederic Amiel

"A woman who is convinced that she deserves to accept only the best... challenges herself to give the best. Then she is living phenomenally."
Maya Angelou

"Men show their character in nothing more clearly than by what they find laughable." Anon

"Small stuff becomes a big deal with sufficient repetitions."
Mighty Oak re: Gnawing Beaver, Anonymous

"A girl's gotta do what a girl's gotta do." Anonymous

"All is fair in love and war" Lyric, Al Dubin

"Love is, above all, the gift of oneself." Jean Anouilh

"All the affectionate feelings of one for others are extensions of his feelings for himself." Aristotle

"In all things of nature there is something of the marvelous." Aristotle

"Happiness does not consist in pastimes and amusements but in virtuous activities." Aristotle

"There are two things that people want more than sex and money, recognition and praise."　Mary Kay Ash, founder Mary Kay Cosmetics

"There is no greater invitation to love than loving first."　St. Augustine

"We cannot command Nature except by obeying her."　Francis Bacon

"See into life, don't just look at it."　Anne Baxter

"It takes a lot of courage to show your dreams to someone else."
Erma Bombeck

"Creativity comes from trust. Trust your instincts. And never hope more than you work."　Rita Mae Brown

"Friendship is a strong and habitual inclination in two persons to promote the good and happiness of one another."　Eustace Budgell

"I saw the angel in the marble and carved until I set him free."
Michelangelo Buonarroti

"Sarcasm is the language of the devil, for which reason I have long since renounced it."　Thomas Carlyle

"In prayer, more is accomplished by listening than by talking."
Jane Francis De Chantal

"Praise, when it is not deserved, is the severest satire and abuse."
Lord Chesterfield

"The cure for all ills and wrongs, the cares, the sorrows and the crimes of humanity, all lie in the one word 'love.' It is the divine vitality that everywhere produces and restores life."　Lydia Maria Child

"To give and receive advice - the former with freedom and yet without bitterness, the latter with patience and without irritation - is peculiarly appropriate to genuine friendship."　Cicero

"I hear and I forget. I see and I remember. I do and I understand."
Confucius

"Human subtlety will never devise an invention more beautiful, more simple or more direct than does Nature, because in her inventions, nothing is lacking and nothing is superfluous." Leonardo DaVinci

"Principles for the Development of a Complete Mind: Study the science of art. Study the art of science. Develop your senses - especially learn how to see. Realize that everything connects to everything else." Leonardo DaVinci

"Look deep into nature, and then you will understand everything better."
Albert Einstein

"Leadership is the art of getting someone else to do something you want done because he wants to do it." Dwight D. Eisenhower

"No change of circumstances can repair a defect of character."
Ralph Waldo Emerson

"Do not go where the path may lead, go instead where there is no path and leave a trail." Ralph Waldo Emerson

"My best friend is the one who brings out the best in me." Henry Ford

"A man is already halfway in love with any woman who listens to him."
Brendan Francis

"For it was not into my ear you whispered, but into my heart. It was not my lips you kissed, but my soul." Judy Garland

"The metaphor is perhaps one of man's most fruitful potentialities. Its efficacy verges on magic, and it seems a tool for creation which God forgot inside one of His creatures when He made him." Jose Ortega y Gasset

"By learning to contact, listen to, and act on our intuition, we can directly connect to the higher power of the universe and allow it to be our guiding force." Shakti Gawain

"We choose our joys and sorrows long before we experience them."
Kahlil Gibran

"Knowledge of the self is the mother of all knowledge. So it is incumbent on me to know my self, to know it completely, to know its minutiae, its characteristics, its subtleties, and its very atoms."
Kahlil Gibran, "The Philosophy of Logic"

"We don't know who we are until we see what we can do." Martha Grimes

"Everyday I'm building a fire. And everyday I train and add more fuel. And at just the right moment I light the match." Mia Hamm

"There is nothing better than the encouragement of a good friend."
Katherine Hathaway

"Never try to teach a pig to sing; it's a waste of time and it annoys the pig".
Robert A. Heinlein

"Concordia discors." Horace, Harmony in Discord

"The supreme happiness in life is the conviction that we are loved - loved for ourselves, or rather, loved in spite of ourselves." Victor Hugo

"Love makes your soul crawl out from its hiding place."
Zora Neale Hurston

"It would be so cool to create a harness, dude, designed just for you and when you were in it every cool part of you would just be maxed-out and people would be in awe of what you could really do." Iggy & Imagineers

"Love can sometimes be magic. But magic can sometimes...just be an illusion." Javan

"Don't compromise yourself; you are all you've got." Janis Joplin

"Well, I can wear heels now." Nicole Kidman

"The best and most beautiful things in the world cannot be seen or even touched - they must be felt with the heart." Helen Keller

"Character cannot be developed in ease and quiet. Only through experience of trial and suffering can the soul be strengthened, ambition inspired, and success achieved." Helen Keller

"People must help one another; it is nature's law." LaFontaine

"It is good to have an end to journey toward, but it is the journey that matters in the end." Ursula K. LeGuin

"Very often the only way to get a quality in reality is to start behaving as if you already had it." C.S. Lewis

"Courage is not simply one of the virtues, but the form of every virtue at the testing point." Clive Staples Lewis

"Fear makes strangers of people who would be friends." Shirley MacLaine

"You can tell whether a man is clever by his answers. You can tell whether a man is wise by his questions." Naguib, Mahfouz

"It's good to shut up sometimes." Marcel Marceau

"There are always flowers for those who want to see them."
Henri Matisse

"When you choose your friends, don't be short-changed by choosing personality over character." W. Somerset Maugham

"Never believe that a few caring people can't change the world. For, indeed, that's all who ever have." Margaret Mead

"I saw the angel in the marble and carved until I set him free."
Michelangelo Buonarroti

"If one should say to thee, thou art a donkey, do not mind; if two speak thus, purchase a saddle for thyself." Midrash, Rabbinical writings

"Even though you may want to move forward in your life, you may have one foot on the brakes. In order to be free, we must learn how to let go. Release the hurt. Release the fear. Refuse to entertain your old pain. The energy it takes to hang onto the past is holding you back from a new life. What is it you would let go of today?" Mary Manin Morrissey

"When you call upon a Thoroughbred, he gives you all the speed, strength of heart and sinew in him. When you call on a jackass, he kicks." Patricia Neal

"And the day came when the risk to remain tight in a bud was more painful than the risk it took to blossom." Anais Nin

"None of us knows what the next change is going to be, what unexpected opportunity is just around the corner, waiting a few months or a few years to change all the tenor of our lives." Kathleen Norris

"I don't know that there are any short cuts to doing a good job." Sandra Day O'Connor, U.S. Supreme Court Justice

"Sometimes people fall in love with people they shouldn't marry." Anonymous

"I don't judge others. I say if you feel good with what you're doing, let your freak flag fly." Sarah Jessica Parker

"You'll never do a whole lot unless you're brave enough to try." Dolly Parton

"Chance favors the prepared mind." Louis Pasteur

"Besides pride, loyalty, discipline, heart, and mind, confidence is the key to all the locks." Joe Paterno, Penn State

"The will to win is important, but the will to prepare is vital." Joe Paterno, Penn State

"Success is how high you bounce when you hit bottom." General George Patton

"He conquers who endures." Persius

"Love is friendship set to music." Anonymous

"What men and women need is encouragement...Instead of always harping on a man's faults, tell him of his virtues. Try to pull him out of his rut of bad habits." Eleanor H Porter

"Don't think there are no crocodiles because the water is calm." Malayan Proverb

"Listen or thy tongue will keep thee deaf." Native American Proverb

"The prompter the refusal, the less the disappointment." Publius Syrus (85-43 B.C.)

"So many of our dreams at first seem impossible, then they seem improbable, and then, when we summon the will, they soon become inevitable." Christopher Reeve

"When I see a bird that walks like a duck and swims like a duck and quacks like a duck, I call that bird a duck." James Whitcomb Riley

"One's philosophy is not best expressed in words; it is expressed in the choices one makes... and the choices we make are ultimately our responsibility." Eleanor Roosevelt

"The giving of love is an education in itself." Eleanor Roosevelt

"You gain strength, courage, and confidence by every experience in which you really stop to look fear in the face. You are able to say to yourself, "I have lived through this horror. I can take the next thing that comes along." . . . You must do the thing you think you cannot do." Eleanor Roosevelt

"Only a man's character is the real criterion of worth." Eleanor Roosevelt

"The future belongs to those who believe in the beauty of their dreams." Eleanor Roosevelt

"Always design a thing by considering it in its next larger context - a chair in a room, a room in a house, a house in an environment, an environment in a city plan." Eliel Saarinen

"If one does not know to which port one is sailing, no wind is favorable." Seneca

"Wisdom begins in wonder." Socrates

"The answer is in thy heart. Thee can always hear it, if thee listens for it." Elizabeth George Speare

"A very small degree of hope is sufficient to cause the birth of love." Stendhal

"Illegitimis non carborundum." Latin "Don't let the bastards grind you down." Gen. Joseph Stilwell

"To fall in love is easy, even to remain in it is not difficult; our human loneliness is cause enough. But it is a hard quest worth making to find a comrade through whose steady presence one becomes steadily the person one desires to be." Anna Louise Strang

"I once read that, in any good marriage, one partner is the gardener and the other is the garden. My husband and I take turns." Anonymous

"After the verb 'to Love,' 'to Help' is the most beautiful verb in the world." Bertha von Suttner

"We deceive ourselves when we fancy that only weakness needs support. Strength needs it far more." Madame Swetchine

"Deeds of kindness are equal in weight to all the commandments." Talmud, Rabbinical writings.

"I hold it true, what'er befall;
I feel it, when I sorrow most;

'Tis better to have loved and lost
Than never to have loved at all." Alfred Lord Tennyson

"Go confidently in the direction of your dreams. Live the life you have imagined." Henry David Thoreau

"It is one of the beautiful compensations of this life that no one can sincerely try to help another without helping himself."
Charles Dudley Warner

"The doors we open and close each day decide the lives we live."
Flora Whittemore

"Sexiness wears thin after a while and beauty fades, but to be married to a man who makes you laugh every day, ah, now that's a real treat."
Joanne Woodward

"The sweetest of all sounds is praise." Xenophon

"The answer is in thy heart. Thee can always hear it, if thee listens for it."
Elizabeth George Speare

"Never believe that a few caring people can't change the world.
For, indeed, that's all who ever have."
Margaret Mead

Appendix F   Dialogue Finder by Essay

The Most Powerful Compliment – 7

Once they finish their story, your line of conversation with them should pursue the talent or skill their story illustrates. Remark by doing a little summary which lets them know you were into what they were saying and understood it. From your perspective, think, "If I get it wrong, they'll correct me and just proceed." No problem. Try correlating the story to their major in school or similar interest.

Me: "So what I heard you say in that great story about drawing and sending cartoons of certain professor's behavior to your college paper's editor is that you really get off spoofing authority. And I think you mentioned you're a Poli-Sci major but you haven't got a clue what you'll use it for, is that right?"

Her: "Yea. Our family is all about politics, so I think growing up with it just made it a natural choice."

Me: "So just how good is your cartooning?"

Her: "Oh I'm good, but I'm not into comic books or whimsical social commentary like the funny papers."

Me: "I can picture you being paid to raise some serious hell on the editorial pages of a big city newspaper as a syndicated political cartoonist though. I definitely sense a strong attitude. Is that an impossible thought?"

Her: "Well, my father wants me to be a political consultant with his brother's firm at the state capitol, but it sounds pretty boring, I admit. I'm kind of the black sheep of the family – sort of an independent spirit. I can't really picture myself telling somebody the right things to say to get elected. In fact, that kind of social hypocrisy makes me ill just thinking about it."

Me: "Oh, well that rules out political satire then, doesn't it?"

Her: (Wheels start turning in her head. A look of mischief comes over her face) "I've gotta go punch in, I'm third on… I think my uncle hates you!"

Screening - 19

Fun facts like his major or minor, class load, where he lives on or off campus, favorite hangouts, sports, music, movies, foods and how he likes his roommate are great ice breakers. However, you should *plan* to move on to the questions that will reveal core issues. Answers to questions about where he grew up lead to important stuff like what his family life was like, and the quality of his relationship to his mother and father, sisters and brothers, will reveal substantial information about this fellow. It never ceases to amaze me what people will tell you during a one-on-one conversation, if you just take the time to ask. Take this exchange, for example:

You: So, growing up on a farm must have been quite an experience. Were your mom and dad both busy all the time with the farming?

Him: Actually no, my mom ran away with the vacuum cleaner salesman when I was ten, and our oldest sister raised us until I was in high school.

You: Oh my god! How awful! Did you ever see her again?

Him: Yeah, she's a corporate headhunter in New York. I really *hate her* for what she did to us and my dad.

You: So did your father ever marry again?

Him: Oh yes - great lady. We all really love her. Her name's Jeri and she's really a wonderful person.

A simple conversation can provide priceless insight. Recognizing this person's experiences and traumas may shed light on subsequent behavior. Crisis weakens some and strengthens others. What did it do to him? Continue to listen and ask questions as long as you want to listen and he wants to talk. Order another latte, and watch the human drama unfold. You may both be witnessing the birth of a splendid new relationship. It's like unwrapping a present, peeling back the layers of paper and ribbon to reveal what's inside. Use patience, care and respect, and you'll be rewarded with what you learn. What's the stuff that this guy is made of? Do you feel empowered in his presence?

The Conversation - 36

Once you make-over your perspective and reorient your focus from "What's happenin?" to "Let me tell you something cool I noticed about you today!" you will be in charge of what goes on in your head when these spontaneous moments explode in your life. Let's just take a leap here and say a prospect comes into your sights, somebody you would consider going out with. Maybe it's a guy you have been scoping at the Union for some time. He's in the food court, seated at the table beside you. You notice a textbook lying by his plate that suggests engineering. You've been practicing the last few weeks, so you're ready... if you can just think of something to say about engineering.

You: "Hi, excuse me, I couldn't help but notice your engineering book.".

Him: "Huh? Oh, sorry. Didn't realize you were speaking to me. I was just wondering how I can get my bike out of a tree behind our apartment. I live with some guys that consider themselves clever to a point of inconvenience sometimes. I'm sorry, what were you saying?"

(You decide to set aside the obvious conversation about his clever friends and stay with your original plan, *him*.)

You: "I take it that by your books there that you are an engineering major."

Him: "Yes, actually the mechanical kind." He grins.

You: "You must have quite a memory, with all those formulas and stuff. Were you able to memorize things easily all your life?"

Him: "Ah, not really. I mean, stuff like poems and dates in history I'm really pretty bad with, but my mom used to really get on me to study my homework. So I usually got it, but it took a lot of work."

You: "Is your mother a literary type, an artist… or a scientific type like you appear to be? By the way, you seem very poised, self confident." (He doesn't, but you're going to drop a hot one on him to take a quick peek inside "his violin case" - might be a major string there you can play.)

Him: "Whoa, you really think so? Actually, I'm quite nervous. I mean not because of you, but just generally around people I first meet."

You: "Wow, it's not often a guy will admit to being nervous. It's nice to meet someone who isn't scared to be honest. Hey, I've actually got to run. I'm sure I'll see you around." And with a grin, "Maybe next time you can tell me how the bike in the tree story turns out."

Him: "Sure, you bet. I'll tell you all about it." He waves as you get up.

If you need to kill some time while you eat ask him about the best prank he's ever pulled. Wow, now you're going to hear passion and drama in a short story that will speak volumes!

Assembling His Composite - 61

Morsel Mining
If your appraisal of his character and personality fit your criteria, make you feel warm and fuzzy, satisfy both your head and your heart, then proceed to validate the role you project him providing in a relationship with you.

You: "I can see the two of us in a relationship down the road." (Admittedly, it could be a short road, but factor some extra time in there for the revelations that are sure to follow his initial sales pitch to you.)

Him: "A relationship, eh? What sort would that be?"

You: "The romantic kind."

Him: "Whew, I was hoping that would be the one – but a guy never knows with ladies these days."

You: "Oh, have you had some ladies use you for other things?"

Him: "Ah, yes! Like furniture mover, bicycle mechanic, jealousy pawn, chemistry tutor, counselor… In your case, I prefer the role of boyfriend."

You: "Boyfriend, eh? Seems like you might fit the part. What a coincidence; I'll be holding auditions this month! Let's start with *friend* and see how that goes."

Him: "All month?"

You: "How long are *your* auditions?"

Him: "Oh, well it depends."

You: (you raise an eyebrow) "I see, and what criteria do you use?"

Each morsel is a clue. The first "audition criteria" he states is *smile*. You repeat his statements.

You: "Smile. I see. And what does smile do for you?"

You and he can have all kinds of fun as you bore into his mind, examining some of his statements and having sport with others that seem humorous to him. You take turns, like tennis, serving sometimes, other times returning the ball. You're learning more than one might suspect. You are learning how you both take turns, how you play together, if he likes to hear your opinion or just his own. But remember to do a lot more listening than talking. You already live with you. You want to learn if you'd like to live with him. What are his passions? Make him fully energize his reasoning circuits and chase around his brain for answers. Is he nimble, alert, quick and sensible… or confused, irrational and slow? Does his brain enamor you or put you off? Is he cute or a slug?

Flattery Encouraged - 83

We're trained to avoid showing off or bragging about ourselves… but we do. I really never gave it much thought before, but it seems the only time we're allowed to get away with flattering ourselves in public is when it's a spontaneous, emotional outbreak. After all, these gestures are just emotional, ego effervescing, as natural as a reflex hiccup and just as harmless! Take this exchange, for example...

Security: "You should have seen Chris last night "lose" the table of rowdies from her section with the proclamation it was free cover and amateur night at the gentleman's club on the south side of town. Ha! They just chugged their beers and had vanished by the time Cuddy and Doug showed up to move them out the door."

Chris: "Oh my gosh, you guys... I was like at the top of my game last night! I'm serious! I was smokin' hot. I was carrying three pitchers overhead in each hand and just blowing through the crowd like I was on rollerblades. Wow! Last night was awesome!"

Boasts are usually stuff people would never plan to say... and yet there's an obvious place for it. The more I heard our staff call attention in a proud yet exuberant way to their victories, the more I realized they'd created a real breakthrough for themselves. It's a wonderful method for reinforcing positive behavior - something we all need and it delighted the people who respected them. What a remarkable combination!

Robust Self Worth - 85

Be certain... There is a stark difference between a healthy, vibrant self image and the sick pomposity of the over-inflated egomaniac whose boasts do not compare with his or her reality. Honest self appraisal is unknown to this narcissistic, self absorbed, haughty, conceited, hollow, shadow of a person. Their ability to engage in constant self inflation in the face of obvious surrounding character deficits is a sight to behold. Do not confuse people who accent their dress with the color red for the matador entirely dressed in red, who for reasons of machismo, surrounds himself with bull. Check out the different types of "accenting" happening in the episodes below.

Clever and Persistent

Security (sweeping) to "Opening" Bartender (mopping): "Hey, did that drummer in the band eat all your fruit again? I could use an orange wedge or two or nine!"

Opening Bartender: "Yes, and you can also have a mouthful of maraschinos 'cause my clever self figured out how to get the lid off solo!"

(The previous night it took two security to get the lid off, and then they dropped the huge jar – wet fingers)

Other Bartender hearing Opening Bartender: "Ooh, I tried all Friday night. You are the *baddest* bartender in the valley!"

Opening Bartender: "I am too, ha!"

The opportunities for sharing "life's ride" with your guy are endless, but they all have one thing in common. You should always be riding proud in one of your shining traits. The bartender in this example "whipped around the block" one more time, for all of us to see in her splendor. She got lots of ooh's and ahs too! That was an "after the fact" example but we all enjoyed it. She demonstrated that she deserves an "A" for effort. She also proved once again how clever she is.

Honesty

You to Checkout Clerk: "Excuse me, but I think you gave me the wrong change. That was a ten I gave you, not a twenty."

Checkout Clerk: "Wow, thank you!

You turning to boyfriend with a cute wink: "See how I am?"

Sensitivity

Boyfriend to you: "Hey thanks for not telling the guys at the bowling alley tonight about that great job offer you got from IBM. I know it was on your mind all night."

You (hand on his shoulder): "I knew it might make your old roommate feel a little funny because he said earlier he still hadn't heard back from them yet."

Boyfriend: "I never feel funny when I'm with you, only thrilled, See how you are!"

Pop quiz: That exchange was about a) communication, b) exhilaration, c) recognition, d) accommodation, e) admiration, f) harmony, or g) all of the above. If you said "g" *you're* the baddest in the valley. See how *you are*!

Reflective Vision - 94

From little bitty spontaneous acts of courtesy that tickle their fancy, to earthshaking deeds that boggle your mind, you practice using your *reflective* vision. Like your reflection in the mirror, you project another person's situation onto yourself and then ask what you would do for yourself in those circumstances. This is the vision that looks at another and sees what you could do to help make their minute or even their day. You're not waiting for a flood or a forest fire to see that another person could use a hand; you're looking for subtle opportunities. Sometimes they require a little courage, so courage exercises are good. The more you use your nerve, the easier it becomes. You soon learn fear is a false prophet. Nothing but joy results from sending out joy and simple goodwill to others.

Amy: "Excuse me, I see your children have you at your wit's end, and it's going to be a little while before our plane boards. See, I'm a college student majoring in Child Development, and we had to write a children's story where each of the children move their hands or wiggle their fingers at certain times during the telling of the story. If it's okay with you, I think I can occupy their time, use up some of that energy and entertain us all for a few minutes. Here's my college picture I.D. My name is Amy and I go to State."

Mother: "Oh, you must be an angel, Amy! I'm sure they'd love it."

You have established yourself in the universe as an intersection for harmony and love.

Index

About the Author

Rick Becker was born and raised in Detroit, Michigan and graduated from college there. He served as a columnist on his college newspaper. He married and moved to central Michigan after school where he helped start a college nightclub and restaurant that he operated for 23 years.

His knack for encouraging people's dreams comes from two decades of working with his college staff and patrons. In addition to helping college students, Rick has served as a Big Brother, scout leader, board member of Junior Achievement, prison minister, separated and divorce support group facilitator and an eighth grade Project Business teacher.

His daughter was the inspiration for the book. As she became an exchange student in Australia dad thought a primer on guys and relationships was in order. A letter grew into a book.

He has two grown children and enjoys encouraging others to "possibility think" their dreams. Rick is a member of Toastmasters International and available for public speaking should your group wish to hear him in person. He would be pleased to show you how work-shopping his techniques can be fun and used as a high publicity fund raiser. See next page for contact information.

Contact Information

Paperback, other editions and documents may be purchased from
our website CampusBliss.com

Use the shopping cart at CampusBliss.com to purchase
other copies including ebook or audio edition.

Email us?
info@CampusBliss.com

Mailing to us?
CampusBliss.com
P.O. Box 109
East Lansing, MI 48826-109
517-333-9595

Use the above to contact author Rick Becker
For speaking engagements, interviews, reviews.

ISBN 978-0-9778254-0-0   print English ed. softbound
ISBN 978-0-9778254-0-1   ebook English
ISBN 978-0-9778254-0-2   abook English sound file

Some editions were not yet ready at printing time.
Check our website: CampusBliss.com for availability.

Rick is a member of Toastmasters International and available
to speak to your group. He would be pleased to show you how
work-shopping his techniques can be a great fund raiser at your
campus or sorority and generate media publicity for your
charity or event.